YOM KIPPUR

NO PEACE, NO WAR: OCTOBER 1973

PETER BAXTER

Pen & Sword
MILITARY

Grateful thanks to the Government Press Office (GPO)
in the Prime Minister's Office of the State of Israel
for their very kind permission for the use of images from their comprehensive
National Photo Collection found on their website http://gpoeng.gov.il/
The cover photos are also courtesy of GPO

First published in Great Britain in 2017 by
PEN AND SWORD MILITARY
an imprint of
Pen and Sword Books Ltd
47 Church Street
Barnsley
South Yorkshire S70 2AS

Copyright © C.M. Cocks, 2017

ISBN 978 1 52670 790 1

Typeset by Aura Technology and Software Services, India
Maps, drawings and militaria in the colour section by Colonel Dudley Wall
Printed and bound in Malta by Gutenberg Press Ltd

Pen & Sword Books Ltd incorporates the imprints of Pen & Sword
Archaeology, Atlas, Aviation, Battleground, Discovery, Family History, History, Maritime, Military,
Naval, Politics, Railways, Select, Social History, Transport, True Crime, Claymore Press, Frontline Books,
Leo Cooper, Praetorian Press, Remember When, Seaforth Publishing and Wharncliffe.

For a complete list of Pen and Sword titles please contact
Pen and Sword Books Limited
47 Church Street, Barnsley, South Yorkshire, S70 2AS, England
email: enquiries@pen-and-sword.co.uk
website: www.pen-and-sword.co.uk

CONTENTS

TIMELINE 1973

5 October	Israeli intelligence receives reliable information detailing a combined Egyptian/Syrian attack scheduled for the following evening.
6 October	Instead of observing Yom Kippur, the Israeli cabinet meets in emergency session during which it was agreed to authorise a general mobilisation. At 2.00pm Egypt and Syria launch simultaneous attacks.
7 October	100,000 Egyptian troops, 1,000 tanks and 10,000 miscellaneous vehicles are successfully moved across the Suez Canal. Syrian forces capture most of the Golan Heights.
8 October	Israeli Defence Forces (IDF) launch a counter-attack in the Sinai, but fail to break through, sustaining heavy losses. In the northern sector, Syrians tanks attempt to seize control of Quneitra, partially succeeding, but are held back by Israeli forces.
9 October	IDF forces in the Sinai move into defensive positions. The Valley of Tears in northern Golan, an area of undulating ground, is so named for heavy fighting that took place on this day, resulting in severe losses on both sides, concluding in a Syrian defeat. Israel regains most of the territory lost in the previous forty-eight hours.

Seated: Prime Minister Golda Meir, Defence Minister Moshe Dayan (with eyepatch) and Gen Yitzhak Hofi (in dark glasses) speaking to troops on the Golan Heights. (Courtesy of GPO, Israel)

10 October	Soviet resupply to Syria begins utilising air- and sea-lifts. IDF regain control of Golan, and begins planning a counteroffensive.
11 October	In combination with air strikes, Israel launches a ground offensive into Syria. Two armoured divisions attack across the 1967 ceasefire line, moving rapidly in the direction of the Syrian capital Damascus.
12 October	Israeli forces moves approximately 15km beyond the ceasefire line, capturing territory deep inside Syria despite fierce Syrian resistance, but are unable to break through to Damascus.
13 October	Egyptian president Anwar Sadat refuses a British-brokered ceasefire until Israel withdraws from the Sinai. Israelis engage Iraqi forces in Syria. Jordan despatches a division to the Syrian front. Egyptian reserve divisions are moved across the Suez Canal to the east bank.
14 October	Generally agreed to be the decisive day of the war. Egypt attempts to push into the Sinai, and in one of history's biggest tank battles, Egypt is defeated with a loss of an estimated 200 tanks. The Egyptian general command orders the withdrawal of all advancing Egyptian forces.
15 October	Israeli forces cross the Suez Canal and establish a bridgehead on the west bank. The Battle of Chinese Farm begins, ending in a costly defeat for Egypt and a costly victory for Israel.
16 October	Arab members of OPEC (Organisation of Petroleum Exporting Countries) place an embargo on oil exports to the US and other nations allied with Israel, announcing that oil production would be cut five per cent for every

A mobile bridge built by the IDF on the Suez Canal. (Courtesy of GPO, Israel)

day that Arab political demands are not met. All major pipeline terminals in the Mediterranean are closed.

17–18 October	The IDF continue their push east and south on the west bank to encircle and isolate Egyptian forces.
21 October	Sadat indicates to the Soviet ambassador to Egypt that he is ready to accept a ceasefire.
22 October	The United Nations Security Council adopts Resolution 338, calling for a ceasefire in the Middle East.
23 October	Israeli ceasefire violations occur on both fronts. Ceasefire reinstated, and United Nations ceasefire monitors despatched to the region.
24 October	Israeli forces attempt the occupation of the Egyptian city of Suez.
25 October	This prompts a superpower standoff described as taking the world to the brink of nuclear war.
28 October	Israeli and Egyptian military officials meet to discuss ceasefire.

Israeli tanks passing the saluting dais at Refidim. (Courtesy of GPO, Israel)

INTRODUCTION

The consequences of the nature of war, how end and means act in it, how in the modifications of reality it deviates sometimes more, sometimes less, from its strict original conception, plays backwards and forwards, yet always remains under that strict conception as under a supreme law: all this we must retain in idea, and bear constantly in mind in the consideration of each of the succeeding subjects, if we would rightly comprehend their true relations and proper importance, and not become involved incessantly in the most glaring contradictions with the reality, and at last with our own selves.

(Carl von Clausewitz)

At precisely 2.00pm on 6 October 1973, the crack of a single rifle shot echoed across the slow-moving surface of the Suez Canal. The shot originated from a Soviet Dragunov rifle, fired by an Egyptian sniper hidden behind a sand revetment on the west bank. Some 200m to the east, a soldier of the Israeli Defence Forces (IDF) crumpled to the mesh floor of a 60ft watchtower, dropping his rifle with a clatter. The sniper then slid back down the dune, with the sun to his right, and retreated quickly behind the lines as an air armada of Egyptian jets screamed overhead.

Officially not on a war footing, but nonetheless in a state of heightened alert, Israeli troops manning the various fortifications along the Bar Lev Line dived for cover as the air was

Former prime minister David Ben Gurion visits defences along the Egyptian border, near the Suez Canal. Commanding Officer Southern Command General Ariel Sharon, first left in trench, explains to the diminutive Ben Gurion to his left. (Courtesy of GPO, Israel)

suddenly rent by the percussive boom of a massive and coordinated series of air strikes. Israeli command centres, air bases, anti-aircraft missile batteries and radar stations were targeted. As anguished radio communications began to feed back to the military command bunker in Tel Aviv, and as the sectoral command in the Sinai raced to mobilise a response, the aircraft of the Egyptian air force began to return to their bases.

This, however, was only the beginning. Before the smoke could disperse along a defensive line stretching from the north shore of the Bitter Lakes to the southern coast of the Mediterranean, an artillery barrage opened up, delivering upwards of 10,000 shells on Israeli positions in just over a minute. Egyptian tanks and flat-trajectory guns were hoisted atop a series of pre-prepared revetments, from where they were able to rain down fire across the canal into exposed Israeli positions.

Under cover of all of this, a force of some 4,000 mixed infantry and commandos, each with a predetermined role, approached the west bank, and boarding a flotilla of inflatable dinghies and wooden boats, began to make their way across 200m of slow-moving water.

Once on the east bank, the leaders scrambled up the steep sides of a 20m sand wall from where they rolled down and secured rope ladders. Laden with an assortment of weapons, most crucially an array of Soviet-supplied anti-tank systems, Egyptian infantry followed, racing forward, often bypassing the Israeli fortifications, wherein stunned Israeli reservists and conscripts were taking cover and watching. The attackers continued on to an average depth of 2km into the desert, and there they dug in to await the inevitable Israeli armoured response.

As these advance infantry units set about establishing the first bridgeheads, a finely coordinated operation continued to unfold behind them. Across the Bitter Lakes, somewhat the soft underbelly of Israeli defences, an amphibious brigade consisting of twenty floating tanks and eighty armoured personnel carriers churned slowly across. Ten kilometres to the north, across the much smaller Lake Timsah, an infantry company in amphibious vehicles did likewise. South of the canal, from coves and inlets dotting the west shore of the Gulf of Sinai, an informal despatch of fishing boats and private craft ferried commando troops and equipment across, while others awaited helicopter deployment scheduled to commence after dark.

Within a few hours, Egyptian forces had successfully infiltrated several thousand advance troops into Israeli-occupied Sinai, establishing a number of tenuously secured beachheads, each some 2km deep and 5km wide, behind which began the movement of heavy armour

The Bar Lev Line was a chain of fortifications built by Israel along the eastern bank of the Suez Canal after it captured the Sinai Peninsula from Egypt during the 1967 Six-Day War, and completed in the spring of 1970. It was intended to act as a first line of defence against an Egyptian crossing of the Suez Canal, and as a series of observation points. It had been established after the Israeli occupation of the Sinai in 1967, but had by 1973 been partially decommissioned.

The Great Bitter Lake (al-Buhayrah al-Murra al-Kubra) is a saltwater lake that forms part of the Suez Canal. It is connected by the Suez Canal to the Small Bitter Lake (al-Buhayrah al-Murra as-Sughra). Before the canal was built, the two lakes were dry salt valleys.

The east bank of the Suez Canal with Egyptian soldiers loading relief supplies for the Third Army. (Courtesy of GPO, Israel)

Israeli soldiers looking at a SAM-2 missile on the west bank of the Suez Canal. (Courtesy of GPO, Israel)

and support. This was the beginning of the 'Yom Kippur War', named thus for the fact that it erupted on that most holy day of the Jewish calendar, which also, coincidentally, corresponded that particular year with the Arab celebration of Ramadan. A most unlikely date for the outbreak of one of the most-storied conflicts in the long Arab-Israeli struggle, and one that brought the already fabled Israeli Defence Forces to the very brink of defeat.

The war was initiated by an Arab alliance led by Egypt and Syria, the latter launching a massive infantry and armoured assault against Israeli positions on the Golan Heights, at precisely the same moment that the Sinai erupted under a firestorm of Egyptian ordnance.

The Yom Kippur War, known by the Arab alliance as the 'Ramadan' or 'October War', was a major Cold War conflict, remarkable not only for the scope and breadth of its military implications, but also for its impact on Arab-Israeli and US-Soviet relations. It also introduced new weapons onto the battlefield, and new concepts of offence and defence that revolutionised the rules of modern conventional warfare.

1. THE HOLY LAND

Israel, to the Arab world, is like a cancer to the human body, and the only way of remedy is to uproot it just like a cancer ... Had we united then [in 1948] Israel would not have come into existence. Israel is a serious wound in the Arab world body, and we cannot endure the pain of this wound forever. We don't have the patience to see Israel remain occupying part of Palestine for long ... We Arabs total about 50,000,000. Why don't we sacrifice 10,000,000 of our number to live in pride and self-respect?

(King Saud of Saudi Arabia, *New York Times*, 10 January 1954)

A land considered holy by all three of the world's major religions can hardly exist as anything other than a land of conflict, and of all the cultural flashpoints of the world, there has certainly been none with the same tortured history of war as the land of Israel. The Holy Land, the central focus of this, and many other conflicts, encompasses a tranche of the eastern Mediterranean intersected by the modern nations of Israel, Jordan and Syria. It is a region of dry coast and inland desert, relieved only by the waters of Galilee and the River Jordan, themselves sources of conflict, and with few natural endowments to justify war in the traditional sense of the word. Nonetheless, since the Biblical period, through the Roman occupation and the Crusades, the Holy Land, and in particular the city of Jerusalem, has remained the spiritual bedrock of Jew, Muslim and Christian, and the source of some of the bitterest and most-enduring conflict of human history.

Commander of British forces in Palestine, General Edmund Allenby, formally enters Jerusalem through the Jaffa Gate, December 1917. (*A Popular History of the Great War*, Vol. IV, undated)

Modern tensions in the region are traceable to the contemporary migration of Jewish people from around the world to Palestine, a loosely bordered region ruled for over 400 years by Turkey, as part of the Ottoman Empire. During the First World War, the British made the improbable promise to both the Arabs and the Jews, that in exchange for assistance in the war against Turkey, both could expect British support in the establishment of an independent homeland in Palestine. To the Jews, this undertaking was contained in a document known as the 'Balfour Declaration' – to the Arabs, the pledge was verbal.

The Allied victory in the First World War precipitated the collapse of the Ottoman Empire, and under the authority of the recently formed League of Nations, Britain accepted a mandate to govern the territory of Palestine. The British, however, prevaricated for thirty years over the question of Jewish and Arab nationhood, before ultimately taking the practical, albeit unpopular political decision, to partition the territory. To the east was created the country now known as Jordan, and to the west the British retained control of what was still regarded as Palestine, with a population of Jews and Arabs living alongside one another reasonably peacefully.

Then, in the late 1940s, the well-catalogued anti-Semitic episodes of the Second World War prompted a second significant wave of Jewish immigration, which culminated in an energised sense of Jewish nationalism in the region, and a bonding of Jewish identity under a political ideology known as 'Zionism'.

A central tenet of Zionism was the re-creation of Palestine as the biblical Jewish homeland of Israel. This followed upon a general mood in the aftermath of the Nazi Holocaust that if the Jews, on behalf of the Jews, took no action, the fate of the nation was exile, persecution and extermination. Under the banner of Zionism, and realising that the moment was now, Jews began to agitate with growing determination for the British to create out of Palestine a Jewish state.

The British, at that point confronting the inevitable collapse of the British Empire, and weakly led by a Labour government uncommitted to any continuation of imperial rule, handed the issue over to the newly created United Nations. A UN commission suggested a two-state solution in Palestine, with Jerusalem as an international zone, but neither side, in an increasingly tense polarisation, found this solution acceptable. In the spring of 1948, making an accurate reading of the international mood, Jewish leaders took the decision to unilaterally declare Palestine an independent Zionist state.

Palestinian Arabs, however, unprepared to live under Jewish rule, fought back. This was the first Arab-Israeli war, known in Israel as the 'War of Independence', or the 'War of Liberation', and in the Arab world as the 'Catastrophe'.

In an improbable victory, an energised Zionist movement seized not only the territories assigned to them by the United Nations, but also large areas designated for the Palestinians. Hundreds of thousands of Palestinians lost their homes as a consequence, and many fled to neighbouring countries – most to Jordan – where a powerful, and at times independent community of Palestinian refugees, was established.

The Arab defeat of 1948 and the somewhat cavalier Israeli occupation of Arab territory established the conditions of ongoing enmity and distrust between Arab and Jew in the

---

Dated 2 November 1917, the Balfour Declaration was a written communication from the United Kingdom's Foreign Secretary, Arthur James Balfour, to Walter Rothschild, 2nd Baron Rothschild, a leader of the British Jewish community, to be passed on to the Zionist Federation of Great Britain and Ireland. In part it read: 'His Majesty's government view with favour the establishment in Palestine of a national home for the Jewish people, and will use their best endeavours to facilitate the achievement of this object, it being clearly understood that nothing shall be done which may prejudice the civil and religious rights of existing non-Jewish communities in Palestine, or the rights and political status enjoyed by Jews in any other country.'

Above left: The then Mrs Goldie Meyerson, head of the Jewish Agency Political Department in a 1947 address in Tel Aviv, at which she accused British Foreign Secretary Ernest Bevin of being the 'chief hunter of Jews'. (Courtesy of *The Sphere*, 4 October 1947)

Above right: An Israeli army unit on patrol in Palestine. (Courtesy of GPO, Israel)

Middle East. The Jews, however, exploiting the residue of international sympathy generated by the Holocaust, gained international recognition first from the United States, and then most of the rest of the world. This left the Palestinian Arabs exiled and embittered, and enjoying the support only of regional Arab governments, and nurturing a sense of outrage and betrayal that is well evidenced in Arab-Israeli relations today.

It did not take long for militant Palestinian groups to emerge, supported by Israel's Arab neighbours. and a pattern of hit-and-run attacks against outlying Jewish settlements. Kibbutzim in Israel began to emerge. In 1964, several of these militant groups formed the 'Palestine Liberation Organisation', or PLO. One of the PLO's key supporters was General Gamal Abdel Nasser, president of Egypt, and a revolutionary leader who had been one of the key architects of a 1952 coup that ousted the pro-British administration in Egypt, introducing a revolutionary system of government characterised by anti-imperialism, and an almost pathological anti-Zionism. Nasser had under his control the strategically important Suez Canal, which gave him a considerable amount of international leverage. His support of the PLO, and nakedly anti-Israeli rhetoric, positioned him as something of a thorn in the side of the emerging Israeli state.

Matters came to a head on 5 June 1967. After months of posturing and threats, and against a backdrop of Egyptian-sponsored PLO attacks against Israel, the Israeli cabinet took the

Six-Day War. Israeli units before their advance in the direction of the Suez Canal. (Courtesy of GPO, Israel)

decision to deal with Egypt, and neutralise the military threat against Israel that had remained fundamentally live since the humiliating defeat of 1948. Detecting a build-up of Egyptian military force in the Sinai, and with intelligence warning that an Egyptian attack was imminent, Israeli Prime Minister Golda Meir ordered a pre-emptive strike in all directions, intended to neutralise in one movement the Arab threat.

Within hours, the Israeli air force was engaged on the borders of Syria and Jordan, and with Egypt in the Negev Desert. This was the commencement of the fabled 'Six-Day War', or the '1967 Arab-Israeli War', an event that lives in the memory of both sides as one of the worst and most humiliating defeats ever delivered to a combined Arab army. Territory was captured from all three neighbouring Arab states – the West Bank and Jerusalem from Jordan, the Golan Heights from Syria, and Gaza and the Sinai Peninsula from Egypt. The Six-Day War established Israel as a regional superpower, with a military prowess that defied the vastly superior numbers and the coalition of antagonism that united the Arabs as intractable, and perpetual enemies of Israel.

In the aftermath, however, an even more deeply rooted hatred of Israel flowered in the Middle East. As more violent and radical anti-Israeli terror groups sprang up, there was a determination to avenge the humiliation of 1967, and to reclaim lost territory settled into the psyche of Israel's Arab neighbours. Israel may have won an improbable but momentous victory, a victory that confirmed beyond doubt Israel's practical existence. However, it did nothing to damp-down bitter Arab animosity, and did not end the inevitability of a follow-up war. It became simply a matter of time, and as Israel established and fortified its new territories, in particular those along the east bank of the Suez Canal and the Golan Heights, the question was less if, than when.

2. NO PEACE, NO WAR

Fight, Arabs. Let them know that we shall hang the last imperialist soldier with the entrails of the last Zionist.

(Syrian government radio broadcast)

Before we continue, it might perhaps be profitable to examine in a little more detail the facts and background of the 1967 war.

The Suez Canal was opened to international shipping in 1869, a project initially of French capital. The British were at first sceptical of its viability, but upon its completion, they quickly came to realise just to what extent the canal would revolutionise global trade, and indeed, global warfare. The British then swiftly declared the Suez Canal an international zone, under British protection, which gave the British almost complete control of Egypt, the Red Sea and the Eastern Mediterranean. This strategic grip held through two world wars, but it began to loosen as the momentum of British colonial divestment followed directly in the aftermath of the Second World War.

India was the first to go, achieving independence from Britain in 1947. Egypt followed in 1952, when power was seized in a *coup d'état* by a military junta styled the 'Free Officers Movement'. This established what came to be regarded as the 'Egyptian Revolution', and direct British control of Egypt ceased more or less at that moment. The Suez Canal, however, far too important an asset to fall into non-European hands, remained an international zone, carefully protected by French and British capital, and British garrison troops.

For its first two years, the Egyptian Revolution was led by a moderate 51-year old major general by the name of Muhammad Naguib. During that period, the Suez Canal remained fundamentally under British control. Naguib, however, was ousted in 1954 by the 36-year old

Six-Day War. An Israeli troop carrier on the east bank of the Suez Canal opposite Ismailia. (Courtesy of GPO, Israel)

colonel, Gamal Abdel Nasser, a great deal more charismatic than his predecessor, but also significantly more confrontational and radical. Nasser was ferociously anti-imperialist, and perhaps even more anti-Israeli. His agenda was, quite simply, the destruction of the state of Israel, and the removal of British imperial interests from Africa, and indeed, throughout the subject world. The Suez Canal, therefore, very quickly became the main focus of his attention, and threats of nationalisation became an established feature of Nasser's public utterances, all against a steady drumbeat of popular Egyptian support.

The issue came to a head in 1956, when Nasser finally made good on these threats by nationalising the Suez Canal. In response, the British and French despatched expeditionary forces, which launched a brief war that has since come to be known as the 'Suez Crisis'.

Sensing an opportunity, Israel, somewhat opportunistically, joined in, invading the Sinai and briefly seizing the Suez Canal itself. The intervention of US President Dwight Eisenhower, however, sensing in the crisis a potentially far greater crisis in East-West relations, and irritated that the Whitehouse had not been granted advance warning, obliged all three aggressors to withdraw. To the British this was a particularly brutal humiliation, which, most historians tend to agree, tipped the balance in the slow collapse of the British Empire.

To the Israelis it simply confirmed their limitations, but to Nasser it was nothing less than an epiphany. He probably endowed Egyptian military prowess with a greater role in the victory than was strictly justified. Be that as it may, however, he began now to sense that it might not be a wholly unreasonable ambition for Egypt to defeat Israel on the battlefield, and to win for the Arab world that great prize of wiping the Israeli nation off the map of the Middle East.

Nasser then began to probe and jab at the Israelis, combining bellicose threats with such provocative actions as blockading the Gulf of Aqaba, and refusing access to Israeli shipping through the Suez Canal.

'We are awaiting aggression by Israel and any supporters of Israel,' he told the *Washington Post*. 'We will make it a decisive battle and get rid of Israel once and for all. This is the dream of every Arab.'

Six-Day War. An Israeli gunboat entering the bay at Sharm el Sheikh. (Courtesy of GPO, Israel)

Such was the preamble to 1967, and, in its simplest terms, at a point when the Egyptian military build-up in the Sinai became too threatening to ignore, the Israelis responded. With humiliating ease they smashed the armed forces of Egypt almost before they had mobilised, and occupied the Sinai Peninsula up to the east bank of the Suez Canal. The twin effects of this brief campaign were to sink the Egyptian armed forces into a concussive, depressive daze, while at the same time elevating Israel's self-confidence and subsequent complacency to a dangerous level. In fact, from that point on, it became almost a matter of established military dogma that the IDF were not only invincible, but that the Arabs were outmatched in every respect, and permanently disarmed by their own incompetence.

Such a comprehensive defeat was, of course, an almost unbearable humiliation for Nasser, and the stigma of it weighed heavy on the morale of the Egyptian military establishment.

What followed then was a period of military sparring across the Suez Canal. It was less than an open conflict – No Peace, No War, as the international press began to refer to it – and which has since come to be known as the 'War of Attrition'. It was an intermediate period, somewhat directionless, but perpetuated by Nasser in the absence of any better strategy.

There was nothing in the short term that he could do about the Israeli occupation of the Sinai, but at the same time, it was impossible for him either to disengage or explore

From Syria was seized the Golan Heights and Jordan the West Bank, both on the ostensible grounds of granting the Israeli Defence Forces operational depth in the event of a follow-up war.

Six-Day War. An Israeli half-track crew near the El Firdan Bridge on the Suez Canal. (Courtesy of GPO, Israel)

diplomatic avenues. 'What was taken by force,' Nasser was often heard to say, 'can only be restored by force.'

Nasser was of the cut to inspire mass devotion – five million mourners attended his funeral – and as such he had to be taken very seriously at the highest international level. However, he tended at the same time to lack imagination and creativity. He was prone to impulse and irrational outbursts. His army, subject to Soviet-style orthodoxy, saw its professionalism eroded by a wariness on the part of the political leadership to promote an educated and professional officer corps. The 'War of Attrition', therefore, preserved a status quo of sorts, serving to keep Arab-Israeli hostilities live. Nevertheless, it offered nothing in the way of a permanent solution.

Nasser, however, died of a sudden heart attack in 1970, having ruled Egypt for sixteen years. His office was occupied by his deputy and long-time associate, Anwar Sadat. Sadat did not possess the messianic qualities of his predecessor, but he was also more pragmatic, and perhaps more politically astute. He also assumed power in Egypt at a time of change. The Israelis were by then an established fact of Middle Eastern political geography, and Sadat was less fixated than Nasser, and many other Arab leaders, with the complete and absolute destruction of Israel. His objective with regards to Israel was to wipe away the stain of the 1967 defeat, and to regain the territories occupied by Israel. In other words, his military objective was less absolute than Nasser's had been, and in consequence he was not wholly reliant on military force to achieve his political objective.

The international stage had also changed somewhat in the years since the 1952 *coup d'état*, and Nasser's rise to power. In 1953, for example, Soviet Leader Josef Stalin died, and his office was inherited by Nikita Khrushchev – sparsely educated, but cunning, and shrewd, and ever antagonistic. It was under Khrushchev that the arms race began, and it was against the backdrop of his rule that the nuclear crisis of 1962 played out.

Six-Day War. Israeli soldiers on the bank of the Suez Canal at El Firdan. (Courtesy of GPO, Israel)

By 1970, however, the nuclear arms race had arrived at the doctrine of 'Mutually Assured Destruction', better known by the chilling acronym 'MAD', which tended to temper both Soviet belligerence and US reaction. Under Brezhnev and Nixon, the catchword became 'détente'. And quite as the Cold War was expanding by proxy to client states across the developing world, the US and the Soviet Union themselves sought to avoid direct confrontation, concentrating instead on garnering global influence through ideology, money and arms.

It is also true that the Soviet Union was falling behind in the war of ideologies and influence that underwrote the Cold War. The historic relevance of Communism against the inevitable ideological collapse of capitalism, as Stalin had predicted, had not come to pass. As a result, the Soviets were increasingly obliged to acknowledge, even if only to themselves, the fundamental failure of Communism. One emergent Developing World leader who recognised a new reality in the Cold War balance of power was Anwar Sadat.

Under General Nasser, Egypt resided very much within the Soviet sphere of influence. The United States had, in the aftermath of the Second World War, been too closely allied to the residue of British imperialism for Nasser to seriously contemplate an alliance. Sadat, on the other hand, less influenced by anti-imperialism than his predecessor, recognised some value in an alliance with the United States. In a large part, this subtle shift in direction formed the bedrock of his thinking over the matter of a future war with Israel. He was quick to acknowledge that, for reasons both of national prestige and domestic political stability, war on some level was inevitable, but he did not see war as the sole instrument of redress in the Middle East. The question in his mind was how a restricted war could be fought in a manner that would achieve the desired political result. Sadat saw a limited war as achieving three objectives: satisfying national pride, shifting the current political logjam and presenting the United States with an opportunity to engage in the peace process that would follow. In exchange for an Egyptian shift from the Soviet to the American sphere of influence, Egypt would require that appropriate pressure be brought to bear on Israel to withdraw from the Sinai Peninsula.

Six-Day War. An Egyptian SAM-2 missile of Russian manufacture found by Israeli troops at an abandoned Egyptian base in the southern section of Sinai. (Courtesy of GPO, Israel)

Sadat took office under terms strictly temporary, but very quickly he proved himself to be a far more capable leader than the local or international political establishment might have expected. At 52 years of age, his career so far had seen him graduate in 1938 from the Royal Egyptian Military Academy, followed by service in the British Signal Corps during the Second World War. He was jailed briefly by the British during the war on suspicion of colluding with the Germans, and again in 1945 for his complicity in an assassination attempt against the Wafdist leader, Mustafa Nahas. Although acquitted, he was dismissed from the army, but was reinstated in 1950s, in time for him to participate in the revolution as a founding member of the Young Officers' Movement. It was Sadat, for example, who announced to the nation in a radio broadcast the overthrow of the Egyptian government. He then served briefly in the revolutionary administration, and then more briefly still as a newspaper editor. In 1957, he was appointed speaker of the then Egyptian National Union, later the National Assembly. From 1964 to 1967, he served as one of four vice-presidents, manoeuvring himself by increments closer to the throne, until by 1970, on the eve of Nasser's death, he emerged as second-in-command. Sadat departed from Nasser's thinking by adopting the essential Clausewitzian theory that war exists as an instrument of politics, and not as an end unto itself. Nasser tended to regard war as the sole remedy for Israel, while Sadat saw politics as that remedy, and that war was simply a means to achieve that political end. He therefore approached the question of Israel's occupation of the Sinai by supporting the 'Rogers Peace Plan', an early UN initiative conceived by US Secretary of State William P. Rogers.

The plan, in essence, pictured a return to the 1967 boundaries, as Sadat did himself, a pact of non-aggression between the parties and a formal negotiation of peace. This implied recognition by the Arabs of Israel's right to exist, which few could countenance, but which Sadat, tacitly, was prepared to do.

The Rogers Plan had been on the table since the 1967 ceasefire, but, unsurprisingly, it had received support neither from the Arabs nor the Israelis. Sadat, however, revived it, and indicated his willingness to work within its framework. In fact, he went further still, announcing that, in return for even a partial Israeli withdrawal from the Suez Canal, the canal would be cleared of obstructions and reopened for international shipping. This would include Israeli shipping, which Nasser had ruled out entirely.

These overtures were necessary, but unsurprisingly, they achieved little other than to stir the embers of popular suspicion within Egypt itself, and in the wider Arab world, against Sadat. In the first instance, Sadat was breaking the mould by hinting at a willingness

Six-Day War. Defence Minister Moshe Dayan (centre), Chief of Staff Yitzhak Rabin (right), and Jerusalem Commander Uzi Narkis near the western wall in Jerusalem. (Courtesy of GPO, Israel)

The Suez Canal was closed briefly after the Suez Crisis of 1956, but after 1967, it remained closed until 1975, which is an indication of the levels of tension on opposing sides of the canal, and the obvious interest of the international community to see some movement over the matter.

to compromise over recognition of Israeli, but also because he appeared rather too willing to avoid an all-out military solution.

This, however, was not entirely true. While the military option remained very much at the forefront of Sadat's mind, he was simply mindful of the necessity of a political preamble. The proof of this is the fact that, while he sent out diplomatic olive branches to the west, he maintained the military cooperation agreements and understandings established by Nasser with the Soviet Union. By the end of his first year in office, having apparently exhausted all political avenues, Sadat's diplomatic language became noticeably more hawkish. This was characterised perhaps most acutely by a brash, but nonetheless popular promise he issued to the Egyptian National Assembly that 1971 would be the 'Year of Decision'. During that year, he swore, a 'Battle of Destiny' between Israel and Egypt would be fought.

This was fighting talk indeed, but as 1971 passed with neither war or decision, the Israelis were inclined to regard Sadat's mounting belligerence as nothing more than a poor version of Nasser's. Bearing in mind the ease with which Nasser had been slapped down, Sadat appeared to offer no real threat at all. A mood of general pessimism settled over Egypt and the Arab world, as Israel continued to exist, and as Arabs continued to work more consistently against one another than the Israelis. At the same time, the Israelis remained confident that a combination of Arab disunity, bitter memories of the 1967 defeat and a proven track record of military incompetence, would grant Israel perpetual military dominance.

The complacency and contempt that this implied, whether or not Sadat consciously acted upon it, proved nonetheless in the end to be the Egyptians' greatest asset. The stunning IDF victory of 1967 had certainly fermented a mood of Israeli invincibility, but it had also generated a flawed tactical doctrine in the IDF – that air power and armour alone, in combination with superb intelligence, would prove in the future, as it had in the past, sufficient to deal with any future threat.

In terms of territory, Egypt, of course, lost the Sinai Peninsula and Gaza, but of the other participants in the Six-Day War, Jordan lost Jerusalem and the West Bank, and Syria the Golan Heights. King Hussein of Jordan, however, acknowledged defeat, accepted the consequences, and existed thereafter in uneasy alliance with his Jewish neighbours.

In September 1970, a short war known as the 'Black September' was fought between the armed forces of Jordan and the various Palestinian guerrilla groups that had established a virtual quasi-state in that country. This prompted the deployment of Syrian tanks to Jordan. King Hussein was thereafter regarded with deep suspicion by his Arab colleagues, a distrust only enhanced when, early in 1973, he confirmed during a visit to the United States his willingness to enter into a separate peace with Israel.

Syria, on the other hand, rankled no less painfully at the loss of the Golan Heights than the Egyptians their loss of the Sinai, and with the assumption of power in March 1971 of

Six-Day War. Israeli paratroopers putting up their national flag on a wall of the Temple Mount above the Western Wall in Jerusalem. (Courtesy of GPO, Israel)

Hafez Assad, a pro-Soviet ex-air force officer, a second front potentially opened up against Israel. Unlike the uneasy ceasefire along the Suez, the northern front was regularly rocked by aircraft and artillery duels between Syrian and Israeli forces. To the world in general, however, and Israel in particular, the Arab world presented a picture of mutual suspicion and acrimony, of military decay and leadership inertia, with the resultant likelihood of war so improbable that it was hardly worth contemplating. Of far greater concern were the activities of the various PLO factions – in Lebanon and Syria – and ongoing acts of international terror, from the hijacking of aircraft to the slaughter of Israeli athletes at the 1972 Summer Olympics in Munich.

In contrast to her Arab neighbours, Israel stood firm and united, her military virtuosity unquestioned. Although unrecognised by her neighbours, she was firmly embedded on the landscape, and could now only be practically removed by a degree of coordination and military force that existed nowhere within striking distance. Sadat, of course, probed the diplomatic potential of an Israeli withdrawal to pre-1967 boundaries, expecting little for the time being from the superpowers – and finding himself not disappointed. The United States, in common with every other observer, saw no prospect of Arab military success against Israel – for all of the understood reasons, and therefore saw no prospect of a negotiated peace. The Israelis felt no need to compromise, or negotiate, and as a consequence no meaningful international pressure was brought to bear against them to do so.

The Soviet Union too was of little diplomatic value under current conditions. Both Egypt and Syria were supplied with arms by the Soviet Union, but in light of these low expectations, the Soviet Union was extremely reluctant to sanction the offensive use of any of the weapons systems that it supplied, for fear that an Arab defeat on the scale that might be expected would reflect poorly on Warsaw Pact capability.

'Rogers [U. S. Secretary of State] thought we would never fight,' Sadat observed during a 1974 speech delivered to students of Alexandra University, 'the Israelis thought they could not be surprised. The West thought we were poor soldiers without good generals.'

Six-Day War. Israeli armour going into battle at Rafah, northern Sinai. (Courtesy of GPO, Israel)

Six-Day War. An Israeli artillery unit bombarding the northern sector of the Suez Canal. (Courtesy of GPO, Israel)

This was indeed what the West thought, as did Israel, and for the time being that fact played very much into Sadat's emerging strategy. Under the terms of a Soviet military cooperation pact, Sadat quietly set about refurbishing and rearming Egyptian forces with modern weaponry. Accepting Soviet advisers empowered to control deployment of his forces, he was nonetheless preparing the nation for an armed intervention, the details of which continued to incubate in his mind. Arab pride demanded a response, but military and political pragmatism limited Sadat's expectations. He asked himself how best he might make use of this universal pessimism, and to this end, he began to develop a strategy of achieving political success without military victory.

3. FORTRESS ISRAEL

We don't thrive on military acts. We do them because we have to, and thank God we are efficient.

(Golda Meir)

If General Gamal Nasser had been astounded at the result of the Six-Day War of 1967, he was perhaps not quite so astounded as the Israelis themselves.

In 1956, the Egyptians had withstood an onslaught from the tripartite alliance of Britain, France and Israel, and although mauled and militarily crippled, the triumph of survival was glorious indeed. The moment, however, was significant for all parties. For the three aggressors – the British, French and Israelis – tactical victory presaged a political defeat, and to the Israelis in particular, it confirmed that a security buffer in the Sinai was essential. Ingrained in the Israeli military psyche was now the understanding that, at the very next opportunity, this security buffer would be established.

On 5 June, 1967, a 52-year-old career soldier was appointed Israeli defence minister, and having served as a sectoral commander in the Sinai in 1948, and chief-of-staff in 1956, his mind immediately turned to the formulation of a strategy to correct past errors, and regain control of that strategic peninsula dividing Africa and the Levant. Moshe Dayan quickly emerged as an iconic figure on the stage of Israeli politics, among a curious cast of characters led by a chain-smoking

Six-Day War. Egyptian air force planes destroyed by Israeli forces on Mitla Pass. (Courtesy of GPO, Israel)

Israeli Chief of Staff. *Rav Aluf* (field marshal or five-star general equivalent) Moshe Dayan. (Courtesy of GPO, Israel)

grandmother, the Israeli prime minister, a woman called Golda Meir. With his left eye blinded, and hidden by a patch, hung gunslinger-style across his hairless pate, Moshe Dayan defined the new and maverick fighting spirit of the Israelis.

Upon his appointment as defence minister, Dayan inherited an IDF strategic plan, established in the aftermath of 1956, that saw the seizure of Gaza and the establishment of a limited buffer zone in the Sinai. Dayan, however, argued that, upon the next opportunity, the IDF must not only seize the Sinai in its entirety east of the Suez, but must act to inflict a defeat upon the Arabs so dramatic that, not only would a regional balance of power be established, but that the Egyptians in particular would be so militarily disgraced that no possibility would be granted of a moral victory being drawn from a military defeat.

He could hardly have imagined how close he was to a testing of that determination. Early in November 1966, Egypt and Syria concluded a defence-agreement pact, following a period of interdiction along the three-point frontier with Egypt, Jordan and Syria. A pan-Arab reprisal was beginning to look increasingly more inevitable, and when, during the spring of 1967, Israeli intelligence began to report on military build-ups on all three fronts, it became obvious that a major Arab offensive was in the pipeline.

Egyptian troops were deployed to secure the Straits of Tiran, which linked Israeli ports to the Red Sea and the Indian Ocean. This promoted warnings from the Israelis that any closure of the straits would be interpreted as a declaration of war. Nasser promptly announced a closure of the straits. The dots were beginning to connect.

On 4 June, 1967, the decision to go to war was taken by the Israeli cabinet. The next morning, the surprise air strike, Operation Focus, was launched against Egypt, triggering the onset of the Six-Day War.

This first Israeli punch staggered Nasser. He had no answer to it, and nor, for that matter, did King Hussein of Jordan or Nureddin al-Atassi of Syria. On Day One, the combined air forces of Egypt, Syria and Jordan were utterly destroyed, most on the tarmac.

This initial wave of airstrikes was followed by a major land operation launched into the Sinai in the morning, and into Jordan in the afternoon, with the last two days of the campaign devoted to the capture of the Golan Heights.

Dayan's left eye was lost when the binoculars he had to his eyes were struck by a sniper bullet. That damage to his face was so severe that he could not be fitted with a glass eye, and thus he adopted what would become his trademark eye patch.

Jubilant Israeli troops. (Courtesy of GPO, Israel)

With a total of 250,000 men, many among them conscripts and reservists, 1,000 tanks and 275 combat aircraft, Israel had obliterated an Arab coalition of 300,000 troops, close to 2,000 tanks, and over 500 fighter aircraft and bombers. To the territory of Israel was added a further 26,476 square miles.

Dayan's objective of strategic depth and defensible borders had been spectacularly achieved, which led in turn to an immediate boost in Israeli security and confidence. The war itself, in which Israel had lost perhaps 700 killed against tens of thousands of Arab fatalities, and many more wounded, could hardly have been more of a vindication of the Jewish return to the Promised Land. Israel was secure, and in the aftermath of war, its military establishment basked in the astonishment and adulation of the world's most respected armies.

The Six-Day War was compared with the campaigns of the young Napoleon Bonaparte. It was breathlessly daring and brilliantly executed, utilising all of the classic principles of war – speed, surprise, focus, intelligence and offensive action – all backed up by solid organisation, training and high morale.

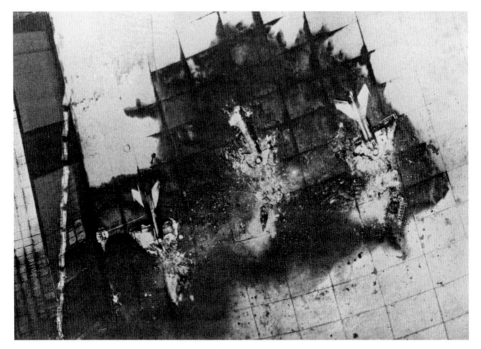

Six Day War. Egyptian MiG-21s destroyed by direct hits from Israeli aircraft during an attack on an Egyptian airfield. (Courtesy of GPO, Israel)

A mystique naturally began to form around the performance and capability of the IDF. Its empowerment by the capture of vast amounts of military materiel from each of its defeated enemies, was supplemented by the development of a domestic arms industry that, by 1973, was providing aircraft, medium- and long-range artillery, air-to-air and air-to-ground missiles, various naval assets, and a cutting-edge electronic capability.

The lesson learned by the Israelis in the aftermath of this success was, on the one hand, that a combination of armour, air power and intelligence would prove eternally invincible on the Middle East battlefield. Secondly, the Arabs were in combination disunited, militarily incompetent, and ineptly led by an over-politicised military establishment. It therefore stood to reason that until the Arab coalition was able to function in unity, and until the various states had achieved parity with Israel in air power, no possible threat could emanate from any of Israel's neighbours.

Of the three pillars of Israeli defensive and offensive capability – air, armour and intelligence – the most important, and most widely respected at the time, was intelligence. Israeli intelligence has traditionally been divided into four main branches, the oldest and best known being the Mossad, or *HaMossad leModi'in uleTafkidim Meyuḥadim*, the 'Institute for Intelligence and Special Operation'. Mossad was configured as an external espionage agency, responsible for intelligence collection, covert operations and counterterrorism.

The Shin Bet, an internal intelligence and security agency, is not unlike the British Special Branch, or MI5, or indeed, the US Federal Bureau of Investigations. Lastly, the Directorate

Six-Day War. Israeli armour in the Negev. (Courtesy of GPO, Israel)

of Military Intelligence, often abbreviated AMAN, is concerned primarily with military intelligence, and the analysis and evaluation of internationally gathered intelligence.

On the eve of the Six-Day War, and thanks to the superb performance of Israeli intelligence, Israeli military planners were in a position to utilise detailed and intimate intelligence concerning Arab planning, force levels, capabilities, deployments and dispositions. A combination of well-placed human and technological assets, aided by deplorable Arab security, gave the Israeli military establishment all the forewarning necessary to plan the pre-emptive campaign.

Such effective intelligence gathering and analysis offered the two other pillars of Israeli defence, air and armour, the freedom of movement over the battlefield to affect a victory of almost surreal proportions.

By 1973, the Israeli Director of Military Intelligence, Major General Eliyahu, or Eli Ze'ira, felt confident enough in the capacity of his agency that he predicted at least forty-eight hours' forewarning of any major Arab movement against Israel, which would be ample time to mobilise reserves and gain mastery of the air. In consequence, all plans established by the IDF to meet such a contingency were based on this projection.

To gain mastery of the skies, Israel placed supreme emphasis on air power. It could not match its neighbours in manpower, but the force equaliser of a modern, professional and highly trained air force more than closed the gap. By 1973, over half of the Israeli defence budget was allocated to the Israeli Air Force, IAF. By the end of 1972, the Israelis could field some 500 combat aircraft, including American A-4G Skyhawk and F-4 Phantoms, and French Mirage and Mystère fighter jets. This formidable arsenal was poised against an Egyptian air

Six-Day War. Israeli Centurion tanks on standby in the south. (Courtesy of GPO, Israel)

A formation of Israel Air Force Mirage aircraft. (Courtesy of GPO, Israel)

fleet, comprising some 550 primarily Soviet MiG-17s, -19s and -21s aircraft, along with a handful of Sukhoi SU-7s. In combination with the Syrian Air Force, similarly supplied, the Israelis were significantly outnumbered, but with a superiority in technology and training, and in particular missile technology, there would seem to be every justification for the confidence felt by the IAF and the Israeli central command.

With dominant air power in place, the next weapon in the Israeli arsenal was armour. The doctrine of desert warfare, as established in the North Africa campaign of the Second World War, places significant reliance on massed, armoured manoeuvre, supported by mechanised infantry and artillery. In the case of the Six-Day War, Israel's lightning advance across the Sinai Desert had been spearheaded primarily by armour, with little or no infantry and artillery support. Thus, in the Israeli analysis of the war, a somewhat top-heavy emphasis came to be placed on armour as the bulwark of ground operations, with the result that mechanised infantry and artillery tended to be prioritised somewhat less than air and armour. This was in the belief that a grouping of the two latter capabilities, in quick combination, would be the most effective formula to deal with the understood strategy of any future Arab aggression. The Israeli military doctrine, therefore, evolved along classic lines of fighting the last war, with the mindset that air strikes in combination with a full frontal cavalry charge by armoured units, would settle any Arab ambitions with the same alacrity proven in 1967.

Thus, in analysis, Israel's victory of 1967 imbued the young nation with a sense of invincibility that, in turn, became something of a burden. Such mystique surrounding the IDF created the expectation that any future war would be as short and decisive as the last, notwithstanding advances in military technology, that rendered a repeat of the old Blitzkrieg strategy increasingly improbable. It was, moreover, clear to those taking careful note, Sadat among them, that this calcified doctrine represented the greatest weakness in Israeli armour, and thus the greatest opportunity.

An Israeli Patton tank in the Sinai. (Courtesy of GPO, Israel)

4. THE EGYPTIAN STRATEGY

A prolonged stalemate would move the Arabs towards moderation and the Soviets to the fringes of Middle East diplomacy.

(Henry Kissinger, *Years of Upheaval*, 1982)

In January 1972, Egyptian president Anwar Sadat opened discussions with his military leadership over the question of mounting a limited military campaign in pursuit of a strictly political objective. The symbolic Arab goal of removing Israel from the map of the Middle East was no longer militarily achievable, and so Sadat defined the objective of military action as simply to force Israel to withdraw to her pre-1967 position, which, for the purpose of planning, included a withdrawal from the West Bank and the Golan Heights. Sadat, however, immediately encountered resistance. The Egyptian military establishment, while acknowledging that a comprehensive war against Israel was impracticable at current force levels, nonetheless insisted on no departure from that objective.

Herein, as far as Sadat was concerned, lay the basis of the current status quo. Like the Israelis, the Egyptian high command acknowledged that, without air superiority, any Egyptian attempt to cross the Suez Canal would be cut to pieces as soon as it started. The Egyptians were at that point years away from establishing any kind of parity with Israel in air power.

On 24 October 1972, almost exactly a year before the launch of the war, Sadat convened a meeting of the Supreme Council of the Armed Forces, and in a stormy session purged his war minister, General Muhammad Sadiq, his deputy and various other key commanders. Sadiq was replaced by the 55-year-old General Ahmad Ismail Ali, a less innovative defence supremo, but compliant, and loyal to Sadat. Like Sadat, Ismail was a graduate of Egypt's Royal Military Academy, styled along British lines. He could claim considerable battlefield experience, including in the Western Desert during the Second World War, in the 1948 Arab-Israeli War,

Six-Day War. Egyptian MiG fighters strafe an Israeli military convoy on its way to the Suez Canal. (Courtesy of GPO, Israel)

the Six-Day War, and as army chief of staff during the 'War of Attrition'. It could possibly be said of Ismail that he embarked on preparations for war without necessarily believing in the outcome, but as a soldier, he took orders, and Sadat was his commander-in-chief.

Appointed as chief of staff was 50-year-old Lieutenant General Saad Mohamed el-Husseiny el-Shazly. Previously commander of Egyptian special forces, he came with a diversity of experience ranging from deployment to the Congo as part of the 1960 UN force, to a period as Egypt's military attaché in London. He was what might be regarded as a soldier's solder, disposed, as the situation required, to follow orders, but to do so with both innovation and flair. He probably enjoyed the widest, direct battlefield experience of the entire high command, and his highest command to date had been divisional. Confirmed as director of operations was 51-year-old Lieutenant General Mohammed Abed El-Ghani El-Gamasi, a former tank commander, but perhaps better known as a director of intelligence.

At the senior command level, a minor constellation of stars was assembled. They included the commander of the air force Air Vice Marshal Muhammed Mubarak (future leader of Egypt), commander of the air defence command Major General Mohammed Ali Fahmy,, commander of the navy Rear Admiral Fuad Zukri, director of armaments and organisation Major General Omah Hussein Gohak, commander of the Engineer Corps Major General Ali Mohammed, and director of intelligence Major General Fuad Nasser.

These changes reflected similar changes at the junior command level, including a reversal of Nasser's somewhat megalomaniacal aversion to an educated officer cadre, which, without doubt, diminished the leadership quality and professionalism of the army from brigade level down. A larger quotient of urban recruits and university-educated junior officers was introduced, which had the effect of improving, in particular, the mechanised and armoured sections, but also the general tactical command capability throughout the army. Nasser had, of course, been vigilant against the development of a political consciousness in the mid-ranks of the armed forces, but by 1972, the risk of a military coup had diminished somewhat, and had been replaced by a fanatical interest in punishing Israel for the humiliation of 1967.

In November 1972, the US presidential election returned Richard Nixon to office, which convinced Sadat that there would be no change in the medium term in US policy towards the Middle East. It was this, according at least to his own memoir, that convinced Sadat to take Egypt to war. Preparations thereafter were both military and political. Sadat was now of the opinion that the greatest potential for success lay in

Former US Vice-President Richard Nixon with Israeli Minister of Defence Moshe Dayan at his office in Tel Aviv. (Courtesy of GPO, Israel)

> The establishment in power after a military coup in Syria of President Hafez al-Assad in March 1971, created the conditions of an alliance that would not have been so easily achievable under the more moderate Nureddin al-Atassi.

a combined assault on two fronts, to the south and the north. This required the involvement of Syria. If Jordan could be persuaded to enter an alliance, then there was the additional possibility of a third front along the West Bank.

From a military point of view, however, it was Egypt that was confronted with the most complex military challenge. And so it is the development of the Egyptian strategy to deal with the crossing of the Suez Canal, and the subsequent threats of Israeli air power and armour, that are perhaps most interesting.

What Egypt lacked in battlefield virtuosity and technical superiority, it more than made up for in numbers. With this in mind, Sadat began to conceive a bold strategy of launching a massive, divisional assault along the entire length of the Suez Canal, to overwhelm the static Israeli defences along the east bank, and to concentrate pressure in a manner that would confuse the Israelis over the exact location of the Egyptian main effort.

Israeli tank doctrine depended on rapid cavalry charges in the full face of the enemy, depending on speed and manoeuvre to deliver the knockout punch quickly and accurately. An assault along a 100km front, however, would be a tactic that the Israelis would not immediately expect, and in the time that it would take them to mobilise and direct their armoured response, Egyptian bridgeheads could be established and their heavy armoured divisions brought across to the east bank. An eastward advance of just a few miles would then be made before Egyptian forces would dig in and await the inevitable Israeli counter-attack.

Depending on the outcome of this, Egyptian forces would either move to seize the strategically important Mitla and Gidi passes, essential to the mobilisation of Israeli reserves, or remain in occupation of a limited strip of the Sinai. The latter would require the steady deflection and interdiction of Israeli armoured assaults long enough to sue for a UN ceasefire

Yom Kippur War. An Israeli tank unit crossing the southern Sinai in the direction of the Suez Canal. (Courtesy of GPO, Israel)

with superpower intervention. Ideally, at that point, on the northern front, Syria would be in possession of the Golan Heights, and it too could enter negotiations under superpower supervision based on current positions.

To counter the threat of Israeli armour and air power, a combination of an anti-aircraft missile shield, a relatively new concept, and the saturation of the forward infantry advance with anti-tank weaponry would provide the David-and-Goliath factor. The concept of tactical missile deployment on this scale was innovative, certainly, but it happened also to segue into the current evolution of Soviet weapons' systems.

In February 1973, therefore, Sadat made a month-long visit to Moscow, where he sought to secure more arms, in particular the Russian surface-to-air (SAM) missile systems that would be used to cover the advance of infantry and armour into the Sinai. The Soviets were not entirely indisposed to these requests. With regard to the missile shield, there was certainly some interest in experimenting with the practical application of a theory then under development, and Sadat

Egyptian MiG-17 jet fighter captured in the Sinai Campaign, being repaired at an Israeli air force base. (Courtesy of GPO, Israel)

Yom Kippur War. Israeli army engineers recovering SAM-3 missiles on the west bank of the Suez Canal. (Courtesy of GPO, Israel)

33

was rewarded with an undertaking from Moscow to supply the necessary SAM-2, SAM-3 and SAM-6 systems. This would create, in combination with conventional anti-aircraft artillery, the densest and most comprehensive missile shield in practical deployment to date. It might perhaps be added that, while the Soviets were interested in establishing this anti-aircraft shield, they were also a little wary of it ever being put to practical use, fearing, one might suppose, that a traditional Arab defeat in any future war would discredit Soviet weaponry.

Here, however, was Sadat's answer to Israeli air superiority, but this would not cover Egyptian rear bases, strategic installations and cities from IAF attacks. For this, Sadat secured the supply of Soviet SCUD surface-to-surface missiles that, with a range of 180 miles, would counter the Israeli threat with a similar threat against Israeli population centres.

Finally, to deal with an almost inevitable Israeli armoured counter-attack, Egyptian frontline infantry and special force units – the first to cross the Suez Canal – would be supplied with RPG shoulder-fired rockets at the squad level. At the platoon level, the troops would be equipped with newly developed Soviet AT-3 Sagger anti-tank missile systems, known in Warsaw Pact terminology as the 9M14 *Malyutka*. The Sagger was a state-of-the-art, portable, wire-guided missile system contained in a 'suitcase' that doubled as a launcher, with the missile itself controlled by an operator using a joystick.

At this time, a joint Egyptian-Syrian strategy began to take shape, with a series of high-level military contacts beginning in April 1972, and continuing on through the early part of that year. Like the Egyptians, the Syrians had been viciously mauled by the IDF in 1967, losing, in consequence, the strategic Golan Heights. This left a residue of bitterness, anger and humiliation, no less unbearable on the Syrian popular consciousness than on the Egyptian. Syrian President Hafez Assad was a Soviet proxy, so requests for arms by Damascus were generally well received.

Once it was established in principle that the proposed campaign against Israel would be conducted substantively on two fronts – the east bank of the Suez and the Golan – a crash programme of installing Soviet SAM batteries along the 1967 ceasefire line began, thus equipping Syrian forces with the same advanced air-shield by then installed all along the west bank of the Suez Canal.

Yom Kippur War. Syrian Russian-made 240mm M-240 mortars captured on the Golan Heights. (Courtesy of GPO, Israel)

There was, initially at least, some disagreement between Syrian and Egyptian strategic planners regarding the overall objective of the campaign. Assad did not share Sadat's commitment to a limited military objective. Sadat chose as the parameters of the operation, the 1967 United Nations Security Council Resolution 242, which pictured an Israeli withdrawal from all of the occupied territories, and no more than that. Assad, however, took a considerably more hawkish view, proposing the more ambitious strategy of crushing Israel between the pincers of a simultaneous Syrian and Egyptian advance, and seizing as much of Israel proper as possible before the imposition of a ceasefire. If conditions permitted it, Assad saw no reason why the operation should not extend to the military destruction of Israel, removing it entirely, if possible, from the map of the Middle East.

A summit meeting was convened between the two presidents on 12 June 1973, where Assad was persuaded to accept Sadat's limited objectives, although Sadat was vague on the details of any Egyptian advance into the Sinai beyond an initial successful crossing. It would seem that Assad was left with the understanding that the Egyptian attack would be in two phases: crossing the Suez Canal and establishing bridgeheads, and thereafter moving rapidly inland in force to seize the two most important Sinai passes, the Gidi and Mitla. These are located in the mountainous centre of the Sinai, which were, of course, vital strategic chokepoints in the potential movement of Israeli armoured and infantry reserves to the frontline. What remained then was to choose *Y-Day*, the day that the attack would begin.

This was dictated somewhat by the tidal conditions that affected the Suez, in view of the amphibious crossing, and the necessity to use various types of pontoon bridges at a number of predetermined points.

Y-Day was so named because the word 'Yom' means 'Day' in both Hebrew and Arabic.

Yom Kippur War. Egyptian army positions on the west bank overlooking the Suez Canal, evacuated by Israeli forces in the course of the disengagement. (Courtesy of GPO, Israel)

An initial date of May of 1973 was chosen, a time when hydrographic and lunar conditions would both be optimum. This was pushed forward, however, by the agreement of the Syrians to come on board, and the necessity thereafter to integrate planning and strategy. Ironically, this delay would prove pivotal in the months to come, and would work very much to the advantage of the attacking forces. This is therefore a point worth noting.

Israeli intelligence organs were alerted that an Egyptian attack on that date was likely, and, in response, IDF reserves were mobilised. This was a major logistical operation, and was completed at no small cost to industry, commerce and the treasury itself, only for the nation to be stood down again once it became clear that no attack was pending. As a consequence, when similar alerts were sounded later in the year regarding a second potential Arab attack, Israeli intelligence was disinclined to confirm the threat, and the military high command reluctant to order a second general mobilisation to meet it.

In the end, the date chosen was 6 October, and this was for a variety of reasons. Firstly, tidal and lunar conditions were again optimum, but also the day happened to fall on both the Jewish holiday of Yom Kippur, when the capacity for Israeli mobilisation would be at its lowest, but also the Islamic festival of Ramadan, a period when the Israelis would least expect the Arabs to mount a major operation. Since 6 October was indeed the Tenth Day of Ramadan, the traditional anniversary of the Battle of Badr, won by the prophet Mohammed in the year 626, the pending war acquired the codename Operation Badr. Thereafter, detailed planning went into effect.

In broad terms, the objectives of Operation Badr were established as a Syrian advance to secure the whole of the Golan Plateau, including the western escarpment, and to gain a foothold on the west bank of the Jordan River. At the same time, Egyptian forces would effect a crossing of the Suez Canal, storm Israeli canal-side defences – the Bar Lev Line – establishing bridgeheads before continuing inland to capture the Sinai passes, located some 50km inland of the canal.

Yom Kippur War. Israeli army reservists getting a tan outside their tent on the west bank of the Suez Canal. (Courtesy of GPO, Israel)

Jordanian armed forces would simultaneously demonstrate along the east bank of the Jordan River in order to preoccupy as many IDF assets in defence of a potential third front as possible.

Of Sadat's wider, political objectives, he had, again, been rather vague. He made no mention, for example, of his willingness to recognise Israel as part of a separate peace if necessary, and certainly not a word was spoken about his ultimate objective of engaging the United States in a post-ceasefire peace process. It was therefore understood, if never formally articulated, that the Egyptian and Syrian advances would contain as their initial objective the seizure of territory, at the furthest extent of which, a UN Security Council resolution would be sought, imposing a ceasefire based on current positions. If, however, the Israelis could not be dislodged from either the Sinai or the Golan, then the attacking two forces would returned to the 'meat grinder' tactics of attrition, over-extending the IDF, and inflicting unsustainable losses, to the point that Israel would inevitably be forced to agree to an abandonment of the occupied territories.

For the Syrians, the logistics of this strategy were relatively straightforward. These involved simply the forward deployment of a massive invasion force, spearheaded by armour, and supported by artillery, mechanised infantry and anti-aircraft defence. The Egyptians, on the other hand, were confronted with the enormous challenge of a massive deployment of infantry and armour across the natural barrier of the Suez Canal, which Israeli Defence Minister Moshe Dayan had once described, accurately without doubt, as the world's best anti-tank ditch.

Central to this combined strategy was, of course, secrecy and deception. Both students of military strategy and military analysts have all agreed in the aftermath of the Yom Kippur, that the Egyptian deception operation –Operation Spark – stands out as one of the most startlingly successful aspects of the entire war. This, however, will be dealt with later in the following chapters, but for the moment, the approach that the Egyptians took to the colossal logistical undertaking of mounting an armoured assault across the Suez Canal needs to be considered.

Yom Kippur War, Tel Aviv. Defence Minister Moshe Dayan briefing the press on the battles along the Suez Canal and the Syrian frontier at Beit Sokolov. (Courtesy of GPO, Israel)

5. THE NEW ARAB ARMIES

Soon shall We cast terror into the hearts of the Unbelievers.

Quran (3:151)

Traversing the world's best anti-tank ditch, although the central obstacle, was only a small part of the overall planning of what would prove a dauntingly complex operation. The build-up of arms and equipment, the organisation of forces, intensive training, detailed tactical planning, and the forward deployment of numerous armoured and infantry divisions, all under the noses of the Israelis, has justly come to be regarded as one of the great logistical triumphs of modern warfare. The greatest strength of Operation Badr, perhaps, lay in its improbability. The likelihood, under current international intelligence estimations, that the Egyptian armed forces would even attempt such an audacious operation, let alone pull it off, was indeed so incredible that even when it became clear that such an operation was underway, neither Israeli nor US intelligence were able quite to believe it.

There were two major logistical obstacles for the Egyptians to consider. The first, of course, was the canal itself, some 200m of militarised waterway, heavily defended and observed on both sides. The second was the sand embankment that edged the east bank – the Israeli side – to a height of about 20m. This embankment had been accumulated during the construction of the canal in the 19th century, and augmented in the years since by ongoing dredging operations. Since 1967, it had been bolstered and fortified by the Israelis, and now stood as a formidable obstacle along the entire exposed length of the canal.

In a worst-case scenario, the Egyptians had to plan around the possibility that Israeli tank companies would be in action within fifteen, perhaps thirty minutes – perhaps with luck, a little longer than that. Both the crossing of the canal and a breaching of the embankment

Yom Kippur War. An Israeli observation post opposite Ismailia on the Suez Canal. (Courtesy of GPO, Israel)

along an extensive front would have to be achieved within that time, in order to intercept Israeli tanks with tank-killer infantry teams as and when they appeared on the scene. A series of concise instructions were issued by the Egyptian general command to the Egyptian engineering corps, which would be responsible for devising a practical plan to achieve what, on the surface, might have seemed an impossible logistical feat. The instructions were these:

1. To open seventy breaches in the sand barrier.
2. To build ten heavy bridges for the transit across the canal of tanks and other heavy equipment.
3. To construct five light bridges, with a capacity of four tons.
4. Erect pontoon bridges for the movement of infantry.
5. Build and operate thirty-five ferries.
6. Employ 750 rubber inflatable boats for the initial assaults.

In order to appreciate the severe challenge that all of this represented, it might perhaps be helpful to consider the character of the canal itself.

From south to north, the Suez Canal provided an artificial conduit between the Red Sea and the Mediterranean Sea, the former being of longitudinal direction and the latter of lateral direction, with a consequent differential in the direction of tides and water temperatures. The canal, therefore, was not placid, as images of it might suggest. It is fast moving, with the speed of current in the north averaging 18m per minute, increasing in the south to 90m per minute, depending on seasonal and lunar variations. A tidal variant in the north of some 60cm was increased in the south to almost 2m. It fell to the canal authorities to research tidal records dating back to the construction of the canal to determine the optimum moment for a crossing on this scale to be attempted.

According to some accounts, an informal flotilla of 2,500 small craft, mainly inflatable dinghies, was assembled for the initial assault, each configured to carry eight combat soldiers in full battle order, with two more assigned to row. The objective of this initial assault force

Yom Kippur War. Israeli tanks crossing a mobile bridge built by the IDF on the Suez Canal. (Courtesy of GPO, Israel)

was for it to reach the east bank as quickly as possible, and then to storm the embankments. They would then throw down rope ladders for others to follow, and thereafter to rush forward with the various anti-tank weapons at the ready in order to meet Israeli tanks.

The Bar Lev Line, that line of defensive position abutting the east bank of the canal, could initially be ignored. Once a bridgehead had been established, however, and as the movement of armour and mechanised infantry was underway, these could be dealt with by infantry assault.

Soldiers assigned to the initial operation were relentlessly drilled in the El Ballah 'bypass', a section of the canal fully in Egyptian territory. It was upon the successful establishment of a forward line of anti-tank infantry that the operation hinged. It was not anticipated that the initial infantry assault would be hindered in any way by the static fortifications, other than in regards to minefields, or, in fact, the movement of armour and mechanized infantry. The individual fortifications were widely spaced, generally poorly garrisoned and somewhat fallen into disrepair. The line had been originally developed in the aftermath of 1967, from a string of forward observation points to a line of bunkered fortifications, configured with a view to offering a tripwire in the unlikely event of a mass Egyptian mobilisation. In practical terms, the line had the potential, under conditions of a successful Egyptian crossing, to be an encumbrance, simply for the fact that it would isolate large numbers of Israeli troops behind enemy lines. A successful Egyptian assault, however, was never regarded by Israel as a practical possibility.

The Egyptian priority therefore remained speed and surprise, and the rapid reinforcement of infantry bridgeheads on the east bank by mechanized infantry and armour. Obviously the transport of explosives and earthmoving equipment across the canal, their disembarkation and deployment, would be time-consuming and difficult. It would be suicidal if even the smallest logistical hitch occurred. Of course, the business of moving the quantities of earth necessary to create a viable breach, under fire, would even more disastrous.

To this end, a young engineering officer, whose name has sadly been lost to posterity, suggested a method that had been used in the construction of the Aswan Dam. Engineers had utilised a system of high-pressure water pumps to remove large quantities of sand under similar conditions. This was experimented with and found to be very effective. Thereafter, the necessary pumps were procured, mounted on floating platforms, and some eight detachments were formed, and relentlessly drilled to undertake this all-important breaching operation.

All of this was certainly a departure from the *laissez-faire* expected of the Egyptian military, and it reflected a determination to leave no stone unturned in avoiding a repetition of 1967.

> The forts of the Bar Lev Line consisted of a fortified line the entire length of the Suez Canal (150km/93 miles), graduating in strength and fortification, but generally consisting, after the War of Attrition, of 22 forts (the Egyptians claimed 31 and the Israelis 16), incorporating 35 strongpoints. The forts were configured to be manned by a platoon, while the strongpoints, built several storeys into the sand, were on average situated less than 5km (3 mi) from each other, although at likely crossing points they were less than 900m (3,000 ft) apart. The strongpoints incorporated trenches, minefields, barbed wire and a sand embankment.

Yom Kippur War. A mobile bridge on the Suez Canal being used by the Israeli Armoured Corps. (Courtesy of GPO, Israel)

War of Attrition. An Israeli Super Frelon helicopter waiting to fly back troops and equipment after the completion of the military action on Shadwan Island. (Courtesy of GPO, Israel)

On 21 March 1971, Lieutenant General Shazly, Egyptian army chief of staff, circulated what came to be known as Directive, or General Order No. 41. This document was an exhaustive and detailed manifesto defining the tasks and responsibilities of each unit and individual assigned a specific responsibility in the upcoming operation, including such particulars as individual allocations of ammunition, weight, general equipment and water. Each officer was included only in the section of the operational orders that were relevant to his unit and responsibility, along with specific instructions pertaining to equipment and training.

The drilling of individual units was ongoing and comprehensive, with each unit and individual practising specific assigned tasks until their execution was flawless.

Of absolutely vital importance to the Egyptian operation was secrecy. A deception operation was instrumental to ensure that Israel's intelligence branches would breathe no trace of pending war on the evergreen breezes of Middle East rumour and speculation.

In the spring of 1973, just months before the operation, and as advanced preparations were swinging into gear, Israeli Director General of Military Intelligence, General Eli Zei'ra, observed in a London *Times* interview:

> I discount the likelihood of a conventional Arab attack. The biggest problem Israeli intelligence faces is to underestimate what we're up against, but an equally big risk is that we would overestimate [and thus over-react]. They [Arab leadership] have their own logic. Thus we have to look hard for evidence of their real intentions in the field, otherwise, with the Arabs, all you have is rhetoric. Too many Arab leaders have intentions which far exceed their capabilities.

This was in keeping with 'The Concept', a fixed idea, not necessarily originated by Zei'ra himself, but certainly supported by him, that Israel's Arab neighbours would not attempt a comprehensive war without parity in air power. Israeli intelligence estimations put the nearest date when this would be likely at 1975, two years hence. In addition, The Concept decreed that the defensive capability of the Bar Lev Line would restrain any attack across the Suez Canal long enough for the mobilisation of an Israeli response. There was also an expectation that, at the very least, a forty-eight-hour prior-intelligence warning would offer the various branches of the IDF ample time to mobilise. Over and above all of this, there existed an air of such supreme confidence in Israel that a majority of Israelis were convinced that, should Israel's enemies have the temerity to launch an attack, their defeat would be inevitable, and as rapid and comprehensive as before.

Therefore, on the eve of war, the Israeli political establishment had allowed itself to adopt a conventional view of the battlefield. This was combined with a dangerous sense of complacency that originated at the top, filtering down to permeate both the military and political establishments, the intelligence sector, the media, and the general population.

The Agranat Commission, a National Commission of Inquiry authorised to investigate failings in the IDF during the prelude to the Yom Kippur War, found Zei'ra culpable of neglect in his duties, obliging him to resign. His unwavering belief in The Concept caused him to adapt what information he received to support The Concept, while at the same time resolutely ignoring the

Yom Kippur War. Israeli reservists assembling at an army base in the north after call-up on Yom Kippur. (Courtesy of GPO, Israel)

urging of his subordinates to re-examine clear evidence that Egypt and Syria were preparing for a major offensive. An example of this was a report delivered to Zei'ra as late as 3 October (three days before the attack) by a young intelligence officer of the Southern Command by the name of Lieutenant Benjamin Simon-Tov, detailing Egyptian military preparations and accurately predicting Egyptian intentions to launch a major operation. This report did not conform to The Concept, with the result that its passage up the chain of command was stalled by an unwillingness to modify the essence of what had become establishment dogma.

The failure of Israel to appreciate the threat represented by Egyptian and Syrian mobilisations on her borders was reflected somewhat by a similar CIA failure, which was influenced no doubt by the same complacency surrounding a similar version of The Concept.

On the day the war began – 6 October 1973 – a United States National Security Council memo noted that Soviet advisers had been evacuated from Egypt, and that Israel was anticipating an attack because of Egyptian and Syrian military movements. Additional comments, however, indicated that that US intelligence services believed that the Soviet evacuation indicated a crisis in Arab-Soviet relations, and not war.

None of this, however, should downplay the combination of luck, timing and astuteness that characterised Sadat's handling of the deception. Part of this had to do with a cry-wolf syndrome, since, in the period between 1967 and 1972, four instances of Egyptian escalation had been noted, and on each occasion a full Israeli mobilisation followed. The most recent of these had taken place in April/May 1973, when, in fact, preparations for war were underway, but had been postponed because of a last-minute alliance with Syria. On this occasion too, a full mobilisation of Israeli reserves took place, and when stood down again, a certain amount of grumbling was heard in the wider community at the expense and inconvenience that these jittery mobilisations caused.

Then, on 13 September, an incident extremely fortuitous for the Syrian deception occurred. A routine Israeli air-reconnaissance overflight of Syria provoked a major dogfight as Syrian fighters challenged an Israeli intrusion into Syrian airspace. At the conclusion of this duel, twelve Syrian MiGs had been shot down with the loss of a single Israeli Mirage. This was a not

Yom Kippur War. An Israeli unit commander's briefing before setting out southwards in Sinai. (Courtesy of GPO, Israel)

An Israeli Air Force Mirage IIIC. (Courtesy of GPO, Israel)

untypical result, and some sort of a Syrian demonstration in response could be expected. The massive Syrian conventional build-up taking place along the Purple Line, therefore, did not seem unusual to Israeli intelligence. Such demonstrations were not uncommon under similar circumstances, and they usually amounted to nothing.

At this time, a carefully orchestrated series of political ruses were put into effect. Different analysts differ on the degree of care, with some offering the explanation that the Egyptians merely blundered into their successful deception operation, but it began in February 1973, with the despatch of Sadat's national security adviser, Hafez Ismail, on a tour of foreign capitals, including Moscow, Bonn, London and Washington, preaching peace and rapprochement in the region. This tour concluded at the New York headquarters of the United Nations, where a concerted 'peace offensive' was launched for the consumption of the international press. At the same time, the Egyptian Foreign Minister, Mohammed Zayyat, pursued a similar diplomatic mission in New Delhi and Peking, in combination creating the impression that Sadat was committed to some sort of peaceful resolution of the current crisis, and not war.

In September 1973, Sadat attended the annual Non-Aligned Conference, held that year in Algeria, returning to Egypt at its conclusion apparently exhausted and ill. In the days prior to the launch of the offensive, he remained out of public view, while the Egyptian intelligence services undertook a high-profile search for a suitable location in Europe from where the Egyptian president could seek medical treatment.

At home, an air of military *laissez-faire* was maintained by the press announcement of a regatta to be staged by the Egyptian Navy, involving the commander of the fleet and various other prominent naval officers. An official visit from the Rumanian defence minister was meanwhile scheduled for 8 October, two days after the planned date of the launch of Operation Badr.

Local Press reports of the chaotic state of Egyptian armaments were picked up by the international press, with additional hints of severe differences being experienced between the

Defence Minister Moshe Dayan, wearing his iconic eyepatch, arriving at an Israeli observation post during large-scale manoeuvres of the Northern Command. (Courtesy of GPO, Israel)

The Purple Line was the line of ceasefire established between Israel and Syria after the 1967 Six-Day War. It lay to the east of the Golan Height, and was named purple for the colour used by the United Nations to define it.

Egyptians and their Soviet advisers. It is also worth noting that, on 18 July 1972, Sadat abruptly expelled some 20,000 Soviet military advisers. Although many reasons have been put forward for this, it has in general been accepted that this was to remove the limitations imposed by the Soviets on the use and deployment of the weapons systems they provided. A trickle of advisers returned, along with a continuation, and indeed an increase, in Soviet weapons shipments, which suggests that the expulsions were motivated, at least in part, by an Egyptians desire to assert greater control over their own ability to wage war.

On 28 September 1973, a fortnight or so before the war, two gunmen of As-Sa'iqa – a Syrian-based Palestinian guerrilla organisation, allied to the Palestine Liberation Organisation – seized a train in Austria, holding hostages and demanding the closure of Schönau Castle near Vienna, which at that time was being used as a transit facility for Jews exiting the Soviet Union. The Austrian chancellor, Bruno Kreisky, himself a non-observant Jew, agreed to the demand. This provoked outrage in Israel, having the twin effect of diverting Israeli diplomatic attention away from her Arab neighbours, and offering another plausible

Yom Kippur War. Israeli soldiers pose in front of a destroyed Soviet-made Mil Mi-6 'Hook' Egyptian helicopter on the west bank of the Suez Canal. (Courtesy of GPO, Israel)

pretext for the build-up of Arab military force on Israel's borders. Egypt and Syria might very reasonably feel that an Israeli retaliatory attack was imminent, against which they could no less plausibly be expected to prepare themselves.

On 2 October, four days before the commencement of the operation, the Egyptian government announced through the local press that lists were open for officers wishing to make the 'Oomrah', or little pilgrimage to Mecca. The next day, about 2,000 reservists were demobilised.

To round off the whole deception, and to cover the mass movement of troops and equipment to the banks of the canal, the attack was scheduled to coincide with the annual autumn manoeuvres of the Egyptian army. These exercises were typically rather shambolic, to which, by then, Israeli observers positioned across the canal were accustomed. Reports of these manoeuvres, covering the movement of quantities of manpower and materiel, were fed back to Tel Aviv, causing no senior military official to question soothing intelligence estimates of a low probability of war.

Before commencing an examination of Israeli defences, and her state of readiness, a brief word might be appropriate on the Arab order of battle.

The total strength of the Egyptian Army at the time was some 800,000 troops, 2,000 tanks, 2,300 artillery pieces, 150 anti-aircraft batteries and 550 first-line aircraft. Deployed along the canal at the commencement of operations were five infantry divisions, supported by a number of independent brigades, both infantry and amour, and backed by three mechanised divisions and two armoured divisions.

Each infantry division included a tank battalion fielding of 120 tanks. Each of the three mechanised divisions comprised two mechanised brigades and an armoured brigade,

Israeli Defence Minister Moshe Dayan meets former British prime minister Harold Wilson, in Tel Aviv during the latter's private visit to Israel. (Courtesy of GPO, Israel)

with a total of 160 tanks per division. The two armoured divisions were each comprised two armoured brigades and a mechanised brigade, with each division deploying some 250 tanks.

Alongside this behemoth was a handful of independent tank battalions, some 28 battalions of commandos, a marine brigade and two paratroop brigades.

These forces were divided into two field armies. The Second Army occupied the northern sector, broadly speaking from the northern extremity of the Suez Canal at its junction with the Mediterranean to the north bank of the Great Bitter Lake. The Third Army occupied the southern sector, from the north bank of the Great Bitter lake to the port of Suez at the head of the Red Sea.

On the northern front, the Syrian build-up was no less formidable. As a foreword, however, the Syrian military establishment has tended, during its modern history, to be politically polarised, and as such coups and attempted coups have been frequent, exposing the leadership to periodic bouts of purges and dismissals.

Soon after the 1971 bloodless coup that brought Syrian president Hafez Assad to power, for example, a series of such purges began, which might partially have consolidated the armed forces ahead of the war, but did nothing to heal entrenched sectarianism and partisanship in the ranks of the senior officer corps.

At any given time, however, about 110,000 men served in the Syrian armed forces, out of which, perhaps 100,000 were in the army. This number could be doubled in an emergency through the mobilisation of reserves. The combat element of the army consisted of two armoured and three mechanised infantry divisions, seven artillery regiments and a paratroop and special forces brigade.

By 1973, the Syrian army had been modernised significantly by the supply of Soviet equipment, replacing much that had been lost in 1967. With the result, by the end of 1972,

Yom Kippur War. Israeli Centurion tanks moving into position on the Golan Heights. (Courtesy of GPO, Israel)

Syria could field, more or less, 800 tanks and self-propelled guns, 500 other light- armoured vehicles, 800 various artillery pieces, and eight batteries of SAM anti-aircraft missiles.

The Syrian decision to ally with Egypt in the attack against Israel required a great infusion of weaponry, and in this regard Assad was well placed. His relations with the Soviet Union were less strained than Sadat's, and by the end of May, the month that the decision was made to participate, Syria had received, or was waiting upon, the delivery of an impressive arsenal of Soviet-supplied weapons. These included 40 MiG-21s, and between 40 and 50 additional batteries of SAMs, including SAM-3s, SAM-6s and ZSU-23-4 – the latter a self-propelled, radar-guided anti-aircraft system.

In addition to this, came an unspecified number of Soviet T-62 tanks. It was estimated that, by October 1973, the Syrians were armed with 1,000 Soviet T-62, T-55 and T-54 tanks. In addition to this were 1,000 sundry armoured vehicles, 2,000 artillery pieces, over 50 batteries of SAM-2s and SAM-3s, as well as ten of the latest SAM-6s, with the usual addition of ZSU-23-4s.

Lastly, one of the most significant weapons in the Arab arsenal was the economic power of OPEC. In August 1973, Sadat visited Saudi Arabia, and without engaging in specifics, briefed King Faisal on the fact that a major war was pending.

After securing an undertaking to supply Egypt's needs, Sadat then broached the possibility of using oil as a lever to mobilise Western reaction once a point had been reached that a ceasefire agreement came under negotiation. This was agreed to provisionally, and then explored further at an Arab summit meeting in Cairo, during which King Hussein of Jordan was persuaded to deploy a force to demonstrate along the east bank of the Jordan.

Oil, however, would factor in to the war only after its basic direction had been established, after which it was used mainly to leverage superpower engagement in a ceasefire agreement.

Ruins of the 1st-century Jewish city of Gamla, built on steep slope on the western Golan Heights overlooking the Sea of Galilea. (Courtesy of GPO, Israel)

Yom Kippur War. Syrian Soviet-made T-55 and T-54 tanks knocked out on the Golan Heights by Israeli forces. (Courtesy of GPO, Israel)

Syria comprises Sunni and Shia Muslims, Alawis, Kurds, Turkmen, Assyrians, Druze, and various sub-divisions thereof.

6. THE TOTALITY OF THE TANK

Tanks being deployed far forward is an indication of offensive action; tanks in depth is an indication of defensive action.

(US General Norman Schwarzkopf)

So it was, that on the eve of Yom Kippur, 1973, 100,000 or more Egyptian troops, and 1,350 Egyptian tanks, stood poised on the west bank of the Suez Canal, faced by a mere 450 Israeli troops scattered among the active Bar Lev forts, and supported by 91 Israeli tanks.

In the aftermath of 1967, the Israeli military and political establishment, now supremely confident, nonetheless accepted the inevitability of another war. Bearing in mind the passion of the Arab sense of grievance, and the lack of any meaningful diplomatic movement over the issues left unresolved after 1967, there was no alternative but war.

Israeli military thinking, however, seems to have been rather woolly and static in the aftermath of 1967. The Bar Lev Line was built between 1968–9, but there was no clear sense of what it represented in terms of a defensive asset. It certainly did not conform to the original defensive objective in seizing the Sinai Peninsula.

The peninsula was taken to offer strategic depth, and not necessarily to provide an addition to Israeli sovereign territory. Utilising the Sinai according to the reason that it had been originally occupied would have meant that an Egyptian crossing of the Suez Canal, and its seizure of the east bank, would have represented little immediate tactical urgency, because the fact would have remained that Egypt had no chance without air power of threatening Israel itself. It only became a major factor because several hundred Israeli troops were immediately trapped behind enemy

Yom Kippur War. An Israeli armoured unit in their encampment on the east bank of the Suez Canal. (Courtesy of GPO, Israel)

lines, havening been deployed with little practical consideration given to what they would do in the event of a major assault. They served as lookouts along the east bank, but that was a role that could have been satisfied without an entrenched system of garrisoned fortifications.

The obvious defensive positions in the Sinai were the passes, and the open desert between the mountainous mass of central Sinai and the Suez suited a war of armoured manoeuvre, which favoured the Israelis. Instead, quite as the Israelis had fought with their backs to the wall in 1967, they would in 1973 be forced to do just the same, but this time without good reason, or, indeed, any particular necessity. The subsequent campaign would confirm all of these tactical deficiencies in extremely costly terms.

The two most likely scenarios of a future war were believed by Israeli intelligence to be either a renewal of the tactics of attrition, or an attempt to seize a limited foothold in the Sinai with a view to suing for a ceasefire immediately thereafter. To counter these, the Israeli's formulated a defence strategy codenamed *Shovach Yonim*, or Dovecote. This rested on the 300 tanks of the Israeli Sinai Division, the only armoured division of the standing army, backed up by the air force. Such was the confidence placed in the capacity of these two branches of the IDF to deal quickly and effectively with the anticipated Egyptian operation, that no particular thought was given to a defensive battle. The focus instead remained on a swift counter-attack that would carry Israeli forces, air and armour, quickly across the canal, and into Egyptian territory.

Against the possibility of a broader Egyptian operation, such as was indeed being planned, a more comprehensive plan, codenamed *Sela* orRock, was formulated. This pictured the deployment of reserve armoured divisions, mobilised prior to the outbreak of war on the assumption of at least a forty-eight hours (generally regarded as easily achievable)

Yom Kippur War. Israeli Chief of Staff David Elazar and Defence Minister Moshe Dayan at an IDF outpost, near the Suez Canal. (Courtesy of GPO, Israel)

An Israeli Centurion tank in the Sinai. (Courtesy of GPO, Israel)

prior-intelligence warning. Even this, however, was an offensive strategy, and did not deal comprehensively with the requirements of defence. It relied once again on the rapid destruction of Egyptian attacking forces, by now almost a forgone conclusion, with the reserve divisions available only if needed. The entire Israeli Sinai strategy rested on a belief that the Sinai Division, an armoured division permanently in position in the Sinai, would either spearhead a counterattack, or hold an invasion. Beyond that, no plan existed.

The obvious weakness in all of this was, in the first instance, apart from the ambiguous role of the Bar Lev Line, an over-reliance on intelligence, and in the second, an unshakable belief in the 'totality of the tank'. Tanks, however, had yet to meet guided missiles, and since the Israelis approached their current battlefield tactics with a heavy reliance on tanks, there tended to be a concurrent reduction in any supporting use of infantry.

Tanks and infantry in combination had been established during the Second World War as the standard tank doctrine of the age, but this the Israelis increasingly began to abandon after the stunning success of unsupported armour in 1967. It was generally believed that infantry-based, anti-tank warfare was less relevant in open-desert conditions than, for example, in Europe, where cover existed from which anti-tank infantry could operate. The use of foxholes, as Egyptian tank-killer infantry units would soon do, seems not to have been factored into Israeli planning.

And then there was the question of guided missiles. Israeli intelligence was aware that the Egyptian Army had begun to integrate 9M14 Malyutka 'Sagger' anti-tank missiles, but this appeared to make little impression. The impact that this would shortly have on long-held principles of tank warfare was not at that point fully appreciated. Some information on such missile systems had been acquired by the Americans, based on their experience in Vietnam, and this was passed on to Israel, but in very few, if any, instances did this information filter down to individual tank crews. The majority of them had never heard of a Sagger missile until they witnessed one streaking across the desert towards them.

Another Arab-force multiplier that the Israelis were aware of, but appeared to ignore, was the equipping of a great many modern Soviet tanks with infrared optics that enabled night

One of the captured Soviet-made T-54 tanks in use by the IDF Armoured Corps. (Courtesy of GPO, Israel)

manoeuvre, which few, if any, Israeli tanks had available. The established dogma had it that Egyptians were wary of night-fighting, and upon that it was understood that no contingency in this regard need be taken.

Towards the end of September 1973, a trickle of information began to reach the ears of Israeli intelligence that large-scale mobilisations were taking place in Egypt. Nightly reports were returned to Tel Aviv of convoys under the escort of military policing moving in the direction of the canal. Aman, aware of the commencement of Egyptian autumn manoeuvres, attributed all Egyptian military movement to this, continuing to advise a low probability of war.

At the same time, the Syrians were also mobilising. Intelligence reports, however, were apt to write these off as a response to the 13 September air battles, and anxiety following the Schönau Castle incident.

On the evening of 25 September, King Hussein of Jordan made a covert helicopter flight to Israel to warn the Israeli authorities that war was imminent. His dates and times were unspecific, but the fact that an Arab national leader, in a difficult diplomatic position had made the effort to warn Israel, was given no specific credibility. An additional armoured brigade and artillery battery pulled from the Sinai was deployed to the Golan, and certain air force units were placed on standby. Besides that, and in the face of evident Arab military build-ups, no specific orders to mobilise were given.

Prime Minister Golda Meir left Israel on 30 September to attend and address a Council of Europe meeting in Strasbourg, where she called on Austria to reverse its decision to curb transit facilities for Soviet Jews immigrating to Israel. The Israeli preoccupation with this issue – the Schönau Castle incident – to the exclusion of a great many clear indicators of war, could only have been of comfort to Sadat and Assad as the countdown to Y-Day began.

The greatest Israeli failure, however, remained intelligence. This was an almost unprecedented fact, bearing in mind the universal admiration that the Israeli intelligence community enjoyed. There are a great many varying reports, books, histories and analyses dealing with events

Israeli Prime Minister Golda Meir passing the guard of honour at Lod Airport before departing on an official visit to the USA (Courtesy of GPO, Israel)

leading up to the war. Notwithstanding a great many general failures, the finger of blame points, almost without exception, to military intelligence chief, General Eli Zei'ra.

It is difficult to entirely understand what went wrong. It is in the nature of things that a litany of errors conspired to create an intelligence failure, but it is also impossible to deny that a more open view of things at the highest command level would certainly have contributed to a more effective Israeli response. The eyes on the ground in the Sinai were certainly aware that something was afoot, and increasingly strident intelligence reports were finding their way to the headquarters of the military intelligence directorate in Tel Aviv. Of those that found their way onto Zei'ra's desk, if at all, he either ignored, or interpreted them according to the view informed by The Concept.

And indeed, the litany of indicators was significant. By then the Egyptians had begun preparing descents to the water's edge for the deployment of inflatable assault boats at numerous locations, and were at the same time raising the height of ramps built for the purpose of overlooking tanks on Israeli canal-side positions. There was no evidence of Egyptian air force involvement in the supposed military manoeuvres, which would have been normal, and the stockpile of quantities of ammunition seemed out of proportion to what would be required in a simple and routine military manoeuvre.

On her return from Europe on Wednesday, 3 October, Israeli Prime Minister Golda Meir received a briefing from her security chiefs, after which she met in closed session with Defence Minister Moshe Dayan, who had been present at the security brief. The mollifying reports offered by the military command did not entirely satisfy the sense of disquiet that a woman without military indoctrination drew from the simple facts, and Dayan was no more soothed by what he had heard than she had been.

In private, Dayan confided his concerns. A defensive posture in Syria, he observed, would see the anti-aircraft batteries deployed around Damascus, not on the edge of the Golan Heights, pointing west. A war with the Egyptians in the Sinai would not immediately threaten Israel, but a concerted push by the Syrians into Israel certainly could. He was unable to shake the belief that the threat was real, and with such words now resonating in her mind, nor could Meir.

The penny, however, began its slow drop when the families of Soviet advisers in Egypt and Syria began to be evacuated a few days before the outbreak. News of this was intercepted by Aman's SIGINT branch through an uncoded Soviet radio transmission. This was interpreted as an oblique effort by the Soviet Union to issue a general warning, or perhaps to dissociate itself from what was about to take place. Israeli intelligence analysts were initially puzzled by this development, and for the first time a note of alarm crept into the general dialogue. This was not easily explainable within the general understanding of The Concept, and although there were without doubt gymnastic efforts to do so, it gradually became inescapable that something was afoot.

Upon conferring with the director general of Mossad, Zvi Zamir, Zei'ra was informed that the Mossad chief had received a summons from an impeccable source to travel to London to be briefed on what was hinted to be Arab plans for war. This was serious enough for Zamir to do so, and within a few hours he was in the air. The confluence of these two events began to stir a definite sense within the Israeli command that the simmering threats of war, evident

Israeli Chief of Staff *Rav Aluf* Yitzhak Rabin, second from left, Minister of Defence Moshe Dayan, in the centre, and the commander of the Israeli Air Force *Aluf* Mordechai Hod, to his left, on Air Force Day. (Courtesy of GPO, Israel)

now for some weeks, were in fact valid. That day – Friday, 5 October 1973, the day before Yom Kippur – a meeting of senior IDF officers was convened, which included Dayan and Zei'ra, Lieutenant General David Elazar, Chief of Staff, and effective operational commander at that time, and his deputy, Major General Israel Tal. The group met to discuss developments, and with the most recent aerial surveillance spread out before them, a sobering sense of realism began to dawn.

'You don't take the Arabs seriously enough,' Dayan is reported to have commented, which must have struck a chord of irritation among his colleagues, for Dayan's had been a lonely voice in the days prior advising his military colleagues to take a closer look at the evidence.

Nonetheless, now somewhat liberated from the ambiguity of days passed, Elazar was at last in a position to start arranging pieces on the board according to his own disposition as a military commander. It had still not been absolutely confirmed that war was pending, but a low-level 'C' alert, the highest alert short of war, was ordered. All leave was cancelled and the emergency mobilisation network placed on standby. This, in combination, amounted to a significant acknowledgement of threat, bearing in mind the wide scope of Israeli demobilisation anticipated in respect of the Yom Kippur holiday. Additional armoured reinforcement was ordered to the Golan, and a brigade was despatched to the Sinai on the understanding that, even against significant odds, current force deployments on both fronts were for the time being adequate. Thereafter, the high command remained alert to the nuances of intelligence filtering in, waiting for the big one.

Yom Kippur War. Chief of Staff David Elazar on his way by helicopter to the Sinai Desert. (Courtesy of GPO, Israel)

It is worth mentioning here, in the light of later investigations, that General Zei'ra held relatively firmly to his original contentions that some other explanation for the various indicators was applicable, other than war. By then, Dayan and other senior figures had begun to distance themselves from him, and to suspect, accurately as it would transpire, that he was manipulating the facts to conform to his theory. He did, however, at the conclusion of the meeting, report the fact that the Mossad chief, Zvi Zamir, had left for Europe a few hours earlier, in something of a hurry, and that things might shortly become somewhat clearer.

While this was unfolding in Israel, Zamir met for an hour with a Mossad intelligence asset in a London flat, during which he was indeed informed that a two-pronged Arab assault was planned against Israel the following day. The source of this information remains vague, but, despite the implications of a general mobilisation over Yom Kippur, Zamir found it sufficiently compelling to forward it by telephone to Tel Aviv. The first to receive it was Zamir's chief of bureau, who obtained it in coded language in the early hours of the morning of 6 October, after which it was passed on to a handful of key men and one woman.

The effect was electrifying. Although the zero-hour had yet to be specified, by 6.00am that morning, a meeting of the general staff was underway. Prior to this meeting, Elazar made his first telephonic communication to the head of the Israeli air force – the 45-year-old Lieutenant General Benyamin Peled – ascertaining whether the IAF was prepared for an immediate pre-emptive strike against Syrian SAM batteries. This was confirmed. Authorisation for a strike was given pending ministerial approval.

Yom Kippur War. Israeli Chief of Southern Command *Aluf* Shmuel Gonen briefing Prime Minister Golda Meir, Defence Minister Moshe Dayan and other senior IDF officers. (Courtesy of GPO, Israel)

In a further effort to deepen his professional grave, Eli Zei'ra arrived at 'The Pit' in central Tel Aviv that morning to again assure his colleges that Sadat had no intentions of following through.

By then the consensus was running against him, however, and he was asked by Elazar, with no doubt a great deal of ironic inflection, to humour his colleagues and pretend that there would be a war.

Authorisation for a pre-emptive strike against Syria, however, was denied. The political element of command remained somewhat sceptical that Sadat would in the end issue the order, but even should he do so, a pre-emptive strike would paint Israel as the aggressor, which would undermine any future requests for US assistance.

Prime Minister Meir continued to work the diplomatic theatre, allowing herself to accept the strong possibility of war by calling on the United States to endeavour to impress upon the Arabs that if war was intended to pre-empt perceived or expected aggression Israeli, that no such aggression was intended. But should the Arabs initiate a war, she was quick to add, they would find Israel prepared, and that the Israeli response would be robust.

Such firm confidence, however, was not necessarily felt. United States Secretary of State, Henry Kissinger, less than a month in the job, was a guest at the Waldorf Astoria in New York when he was abruptly awakened at 6.15am by his deputy to be informed that war was about to break out in the Middle East. This marked the commencement of a memorable day. While reading Mrs. Meir's hawkish public pronouncements, he was also granted an insight into her personal anxieties by an admission in private that Israel might be in trouble. Kissinger immediately contacted the Soviet ambassador to Washington, Anatoly Dobrynin, with whom he shared Israel's assurances that no Israeli offensive was planned, requesting that Moscow be alerted. He further asked that that these sentiments be passed on to the presidents of Egypt and Syria. Kissinger then placed a telephone call to the Israeli chargé d'affaires in Washington, informing him of his conversation with Dobrynin, and urging the Israelis not to do nothing rash.

At noon, an emergency cabinet meeting was convened in Tel Aviv. Prime Minister Meir revealed that an impeccable source, perhaps the Israeli Foreign Minister Abba Eban, who was then in New York attending the 28th session of the UN General Assembly, had revealed that hostilities would break out at 6.00pm that day. As a civilian Meir's instincts had for some time

---

'The Source', as Zamir referred to him, is indicated in some sources as Ashraf Marwan, a son-in-law of Gamal Nasser and Sadat's information secretary..

According to Edgar O'Ballance, a highly respected Irish defence reporter, analyst and academic, whose book *No Victor, No Vanquished*, remains one of the most quoted coverages of the Yom Kippur War, the information was received from the Israeli Foreign Minister, then in New York. To quote from *No Victor. No Vanquished*, O'Ballance writes: 'At approximately 4:00 A.M. (Israeli time) on 6 October, Premier Meir received a signal which Abba Eban, the Israeli foreign minister, then in New York, had dispatched at 9:00 P.M. (New York time) the previous day, there being a time difference of seven hours.'

'The Pit' was, and is, the Israeli military command centre located at the Kirya military headquarters in Tel Aviv.

Yom Kippur War. Israeli Prime Minister Golda Meir, Chief of Staff David Elazar and *Aluf* Shmuel Gonen visiting an IDF Southern Command outpost in the Sinai. (Courtesy of GPO, Israel)

been leaning in the direction of war, and at this point, notwithstanding a lingering residue of scepticism among the military men, she was now inclined to take the warnings seriously. The hour was crucial, for if the Israelis anticipated the outbreak at 6.00pm, they were poised to be surprised. Zero-hour was 2.00pm, four hours earlier than anticipated, and those four hours would prove to be critical.

A few minutes before 2.00pm, Egyptian President Anwar Sadat entered Centre 10, the Egyptian command centre located in Cairo, where he took his seat for the commencement of Operation Badr.

Across the Suez Canal, Israeli troops manning the Bar Lev Forts were placed on alert, and told to don their helmets and flak-jackets while observers at the base of Mount Hermon reported that Syrian tanks were being stripped of their camouflage netting. Signs of a major mobilisation were now unmistakeable.

In the cabinet room in Tel Aviv, Defence Minister Moshi Dayan was wrapping up his brief when an aide entered the room and handed him a note. Reading the note his face blanched. He looked up and surveyed his expectant colleagues. The room was thick with cigarette smoke. Egyptian warplanes, he announced, were attacking Israeli positions in the Sinai. The war had begun.

Prime Minister Meir, a cigarette poised at her lips, her grey hair dishevelled and dark rings under her eyes, stared into the middle distance for no more than a second or two before drawing the meeting abruptly to a close.

Outside in the streets there was an uncanny silence before, in the distance, there rose the morbid wail of a siren, and then another.

7. WAR

But we could not avoid showing at once that the bloody solution of the crisis, the effort for the destruction of the enemy's force, is the firstborn son of war.

(Karl von Clausewitz)

At 1.45pm, on 6 October 1973, having attended the sombre general staff meeting in Tel Aviv, chief of the Southern Command, General Shmuel Gonen, contacted his divisional commander, Major General Avraham Mandler. After a general review of orders, Gonen suggested that Mandler begin moving his armoured brigades closer to the front, to which Mandler, in one of the most frequently cited utterances of the war, agreed: 'Yes,' he said, 'I suppose we had. We are being bombed at this moment.'

This laconic observation came moments before a deluge of radio traffic, originating from the various strongpoints along the Bar Lev Line, confirmed that a major assault was indeed underway. Heavy fighting was reported at each of the various manned forts, most occupied by reservists of the Jerusalem Brigade. In some instances junior NCOs were in command, the officers having been killed in the first wave.

To the Israeli high command buried in 'The Pit', the news came as a shock, but the confusion surrounding the situation was entirely one-sided. In Centre 10, 250km to the west, in the centre of Cairo, Egyptian President Anwar Sadat was observing with satisfaction the performance of the coordinating command, and reading with a sense of reserved confidence the moment-by-moment reports of the assault underway. The facts of the launch of Operation Badr on the Sinai front are simple. The curtain of secrecy and deception behind the movement of five divisions to the west bank of the Suez Canal was dropped when waves of Egyptian aircraft skimmed across the deceptively placid surface of the canal and unleashed a firestorm on Israeli strategic positions in the Sinai. This included airfields, command facilities, and artillery and anti-aircraft installations.

At precisely the same moment, 2,000 guns opened up along the entire front, delivering their payload of 10,000 shells of various ordnances on the stunned Israelis, who for the most part had anticipated another four hours to mobilise before the expected onslaught. As the opening barrage was underway, the initial crossing began.

By 2.15pm, as the first aircraft were returning, the initial assault wave was poised to take to their boats and begin a superbly ordered crossing that had been practised and rehearsed hundreds of times – the results of this showed. Approximately 8,000 Egyptian infantrymen

Major General Mandler's command was the 252nd Armoured Division.
It was estimated by Egyptian military planners that the cost in casualties during the initial crossing would run to between 25,000 and 30,000, with 10,000 fatalities, but in the event, only 208 were reported killed, which stunned even the Egyptians themselves.

surged across the canal along its full length, reaching the east bank, in most cases, in formation. Where resistance was encountered, it was for the most part light and disorganised.

Egyptian casualties, anticipated to be high, proved in fact to be lower than the most optimistic assessments. As the first craft approached the east bank, troops swarmed up the sand embankments, dropping rope ladders for their comrades. Commando and tank-killer units then pushed forward, bypassing the fortifications, mining tank ramps and preparing anti-tank ambushes, and waiting thereafter for the inevitable appearance of Israeli armour.

As this was underway, bridge-laying teams began assembling a series of mobile bridge systems, some for crossing tanks, and others for infantry. Ten bridges were ultimately deployed, concentrated in three areas – to the north, around the settlement of Kantara, centrally at Ismailia-Devesoir, and to the south near Geneifa-Suez.

Yom Kippur War. Israeli army reservists stationed on the west bank of the Suez Canal calling their families. (Courtesy of GPO, Israel)

Simultaneously, a flotilla of floating water-cannon took to the water and were soon blasting the sand embankments with high-pressure hoses. Within two or three hours, access breaches began to come into commission, and the divisions began their orderly crossing.

In one or two places, the embankments were composed, not of sand, but a finer clay, and instead of melting away under high-pressure hoses, the earth subsidised and settled into a muddy quagmire. The pump crews were singled out for attention by the Israeli defence, and the highest per-capita casualties on the Egyptian side were recorded among them.

Overhead, the Israeli air force put in an appearance, menacing the bridges before the aircraft were driven back, sustaining casualties from the Egyptian anti-aircraft shield.

As the divisions crossed in four- to five-mile sectors, the first incoming tanks secured the crossing zone. The second wave moved out to about 150m where they established positions before being joined over the next few hours by the third and fourth waves.

By then the first wave of invasion troops had reached a depth of 2.5km, where they dug in, preparing for the Israeli tank advance. Farther south, commandos and special forces were deploying in depth by helicopter, but as these pushed beyond the protection of the Egyptian anti-aircraft shield, the IAF moved in. In total, fourteen Egyptian helicopters were shot down.

Across the Great Bitter Lake, a shallow, inland expanse of salt water, an Egyptian marine brigade began a more traditional amphibious crossing, penetrating a largely undefended

An Israeli Air Force American-made F-4 Phantom. (Courtesy of GPO, Israel)

front, before striking inland to rendezvous with commando troops at the Mitla and Gidi passes, where they would harass and interdict Israeli military traffic.

Arriving on the east bank a little behind the first assault waves, detachments of infantry, specially trained for the task, began to engage the fortifications. As they did, distressed calls began to be registered at the Southern Command HQ, pleading for air and armoured reinforcements. These were promised, but the Israeli Southern Command Headquarters, based at Beersheba to the south of Jerusalem, was inundated with such calls and reports, and for the moment could formulate no clear picture of what was taking place.

Before very long, within two hours in fact, Egyptians flags were hoisted above a handful of the sixteen defended Bar Lev Line fortifications, and their Israeli defenders taken prisoner. The remainder, though continuing to bear the brunt, held out – for the time being at least.

The deficiencies of the Bar Lev line became immediately obvious to those observing the situation unfold. The question soon became one not of their capacity to defend the Suez line, but whether to implement a push to relieve them or not. Indeed, it was the desperate circumstances of many of these frontline fortifications that inspired the initial Israeli tank charges that would prove so costly in the opening phases of the war.

General Gonen, at this time pacing the floor of his control room, plotted the flood of reports coming in from the front, trying from them to gain a clear picture of the forming battlefield. Within two or three hours of the commencement of the Egyptian assault, it became clear to him that a major amphibious operation was underway along the entire length of the canal. There was, however, no immediately identifiable 'main effort'.

As a conventional soldier, Gonan was somewhat limited by doctrine – current doctrine decreed an inevitable 'main effort' along a line of conventional attack. With the limited response capability of three dispersed tank brigades, he could not respond to an extended front, and so it was essential that he identify the specific sector where the Egyptians would focus their main assault. As mentioned earlier, current Israeli thinking contained in the

Yom Kippur War. Israeli *Aluf* Arik Sharon and Chief of Southern Command *Aluf* Shmuel Gonen, far right, at an IDF outpost in the Sinai. (Courtesy of GPO, Israel)

Dovecote strategy narrowed the potential Israeli response to a rapid and overwhelming armoured assault, with the IAF in support. This required, as an essential element, a specific point upon which to focus an assault, as the conclusion would be a lightning crossing of the Suez followed by a rapid advance into Egyptian territory.

These shock tactics, however, were not configured to cope with a dispersed assault in equal strength along a 100km front. The commander of the Sinai Division, Major General Mandler, having been forewarned of the Egyptian attack expected at 6.00pm, ordered an armoured advance on the canal. In accordance with Dovecote, this had to be concluded no earlier than 4.00pm, and no later than 5.00pm. However, with the opening of the assault at 2.00pm, four hours earlier than anticipated, the three tank battalions were taken unaware, and their deployment, therefore, was somewhat hurried and ill considered.

The three armoured brigades of the Sinai Division – under the respective commands of colonels Gaby Amir to the north, Amnon Reshef at the centre, and Dan Shomron farther south – were deployed to the east of the Lateral Road, one of three Israeli military roads that ran north to south and broadly parallel with the canal. The first of these roads was the Canal Road, running more or less along the east bank of the canal, and linking the fortified positions of the Bar Lev Line. The second was the the Artillery Road, about 10km farther inland. The third, the Lateral Road, or Supply Road, was 20km farther inland still. These roads had been either built or improved as part of the Bar Lev complex, providing a medium for the rapid movement and deployment of land forces on the western edge of the Sinai. These roads were intersected by four east–west lateral roads, the first in the north, which plied open desert, and three farther to the south, utilising passes through the mountainous mass of the south–central Sinai.

Israeli Defence Minister Moshe Dayan with senior officers at an observation post during manoeuvres of the Northern Command. (Courtesy of GPO, Israel)

Lying 10km or so back from the canal, and spaced out along the whole front, were six fortified Israeli command posts – camouflaged and well protected, each controlling their respective areas. The main military installation in the Sinai was situated about 50km from the canal, at Bir Gifgafa, known by the Israelis as Refidim, where a large military complex contained the HQ of Southern Command.

It was from here that Mandler, after the initial wave of air attacks, ordered a cautious advance on the canal, despite there being no clear picture of what was taking place. No advance reconnaissance had been ordered, however, and Israeli tanks, as they approached the canal with the afternoon sun in their eyes, were met by teams of Egyptian tank-killers, who stepped out of their foxholes, firing Sagger missiles, followed by walls of RPG rockets. From ramparts on the west bank of the canal, Egyptian tanks had been pre-positioned to engage the approaching Israelis, who, in almost all respects, blundered into carefully prepared Egyptian ambushes.

In all cases, the Israeli objective was broadly to link up with fortifications of the Bar Lev Line, and although all three brigades pushed forward to pre-prepared positions, all three, most particularly those of Reshef and Shomron, and in each case critically outnumbered, fought ferocious battles against Egyptian armour and infantry. All three encountered a degree of ferocity and commitment in battle from the Egyptians, and although a heavy price was exacted on Egyptian tanks and infantry personnel, they held their lines. The IAF, that major pillar of Dovecote, was deterred by the Egyptian anti-aircraft shield. Although they mounted 120 sorties during the course of the first day, little was achieved in what were in effect lightning, snap attacks that did not amount to effective ground support.

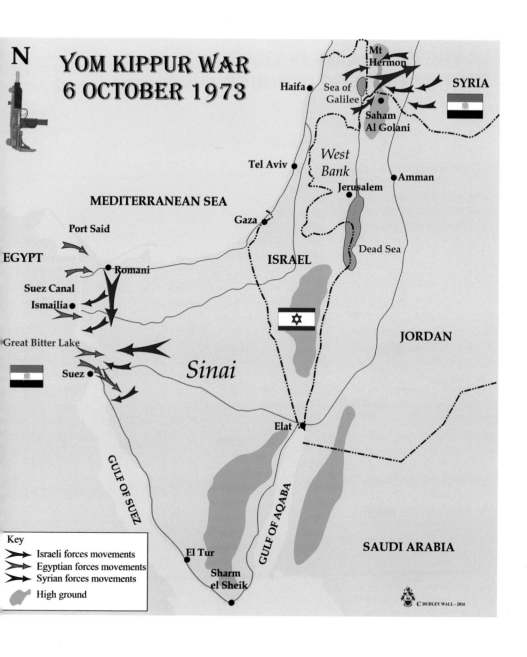

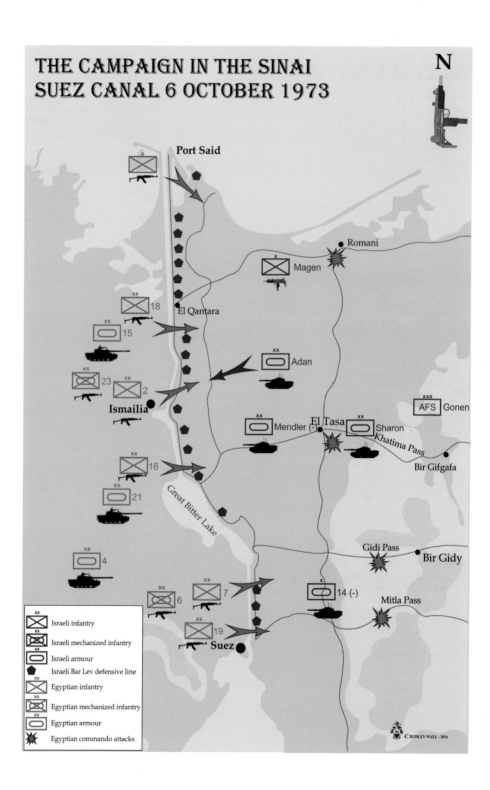

THE CAMPAIGN IN THE SINAI
SUEZ CANAL 6 OCTOBER 1973

N

Port Said

Romani

Magen

El Qantara

18

15

Adan

23 2

Ismailia

Mendler (-) El Tasa Sharon

AFS Gonen

Khatima Pass

Bir Gifgafa

16

21

Great Bitter Lake

4

Gidi Pass Bir Gidy

6 7 14 (-) Mitla Pass

19 Suez

Israeli infantry	
Israeli mechanized infantry	
Israeli armour	
Israeli Bar Lev defensive line	
Egyptian infantry	
Egyptian mechanized infantry	
Egyptian armour	
Egyptian commando attacks	

C DUDLEY WALL - 2016

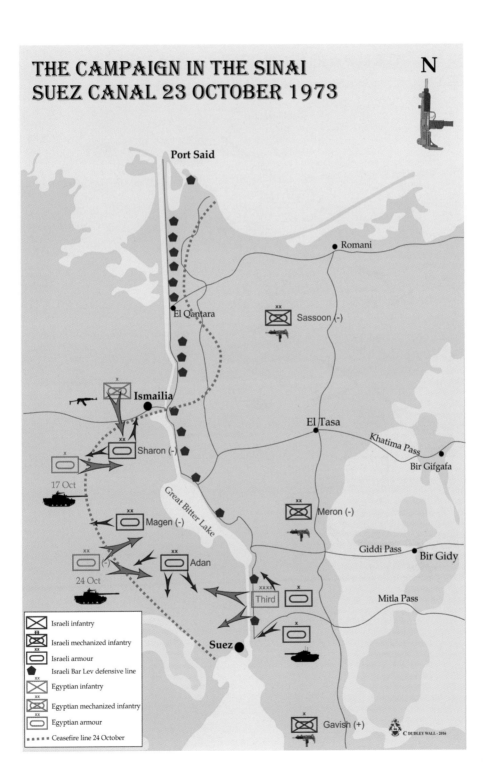

THE CAMPAIGN IN THE SINAI
SUEZ CANAL 23 OCTOBER 1973

N

Port Said

Romani

El Qantara

Sassoon (-)

Ismailia

El Tasa

Khatima Pass

Bir Gifgafa

Sharon (-)

17 Oct

Great Bitter Lake

Magen (-)

Meron (-)

Giddi Pass

Bir Gidy

Adan

24 Oct

Third

Mitla Pass

Suez

Legend:
- Israeli infantry
- Israeli mechanized infantry
- Israeli armour
- Israeli Bar Lev defensive line
- Egyptian infantry
- Egyptian mechanized infantry
- Egyptian armour
- Ceasefire line 24 October

Gavish (+)

C DUDLEY WALL - 2016

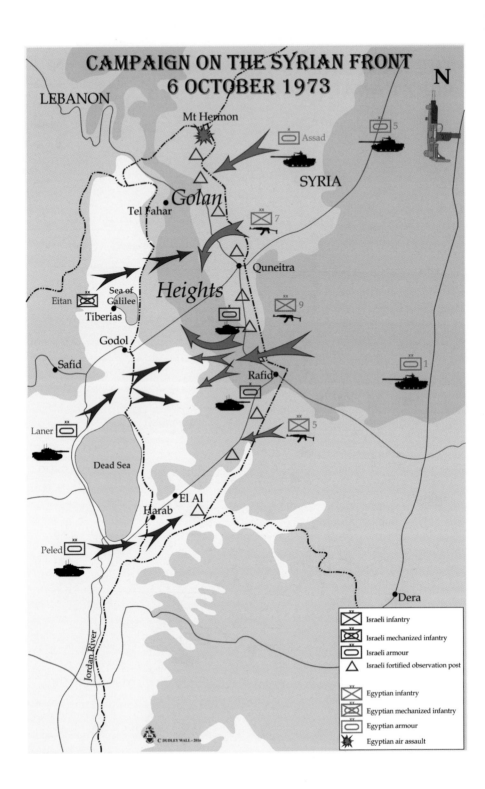

CAMPAIGN ON THE SYRIAN FRONT
6 OCTOBER 1973

N

LEBANON

Mt Hermon

Assad

SYRIA

Golan

Tel Fahar

7

Heights

Quneitra

Eitan

Sea of
Galilee

Tiberias

9

Godol

1

Safid

Rafid

Laner

5

Dead Sea

El Al

Harab

Peled

Dera

Jordan River

C DUDLEY WALL - 2016

	Israeli infantry
	Israeli mechanized infantry
	Israeli armour
△	Israeli fortified observation post
	Egyptian infantry
	Egyptian mechanized infantry
	Egyptian armour
	Egyptian air assault

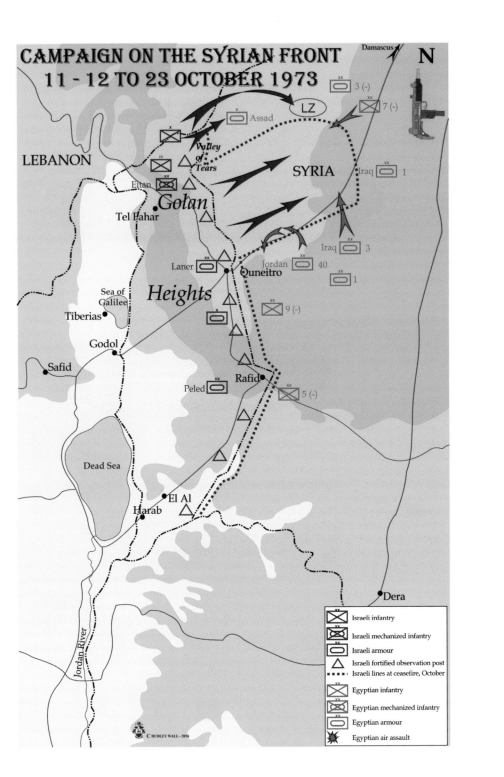

CAMPAIGN ON THE SYRIAN FRONT
11 - 12 TO 23 OCTOBER 1973

Damascus

N

3 (-)

7 (-)

Assad

LZ

Valley of Tears

LEBANON

Eitan

SYRIA

Iraq 1

Golan

Tel Fahar

Laner

Quneitro

Jordan 40

Iraq 3

1

Heights

Sea of Galilee

Tiberias

9 (-)

Godol

Safid

Rafid

Peled

5 (-)

Dead Sea

El Al

Harab

Jordan River

Dera

Israeli infantry	
Israeli mechanized infantry	
Israeli armour	
Israeli fortified observation post	
Israeli lines at ceasefire, October	
Egyptian infantry	
Egyptian mechanized infantry	
Egyptian armour	
Egyptian air assault	

C DUDLEY WALL - 2016

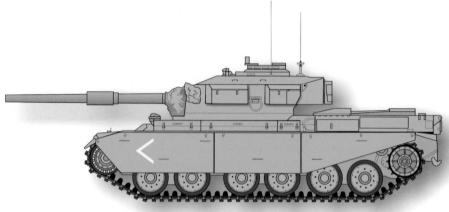

Israeli Centurion tank of the 7th Armoured Brigade on the Golan Heights

Egyptian T-54 A tank

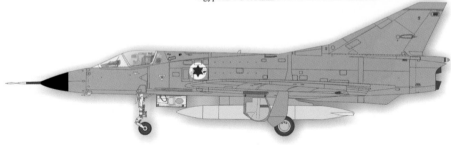

Israeli Mirage III

Syrian MiG-21

Israeli Armoured Corps memorial on the Golan Heights to their soldiers who fell in the Yom Kippur War.

Israeli Patton M-48 tanks on parade after the evacuation from Refidim in the Sinai as a result of the ceasefire.

Israeli Air Force McDonnell Douglas F-4 Phantom with its potential payload of ordnance.

Israeli Air Force Dassault Mirage III armed and on standby for deployment.

Israeli Air Force McDonnell Douglas F-4 Phantom.

Israeli Air Force Lockheed C-130 Hercules.

Israeli Air Force Aérospatiale SA.321 Super Frelon.

Israeli Raytheon MIM-23 Hawk ground-to-air missile system.

Israeli Air Force Lockheed C-130 Hercules.

Israeli Air Force McDonnell Douglas F-4 Phantom.

Israeli Air Force Dassault Mirage III.

Israeli Air Force McDonnell Douglas A-4 Skyhawks.

An Israeli Air Force American-built McDonnell Douglas A-4 Skyhawk. (Courtesy of GPO, Israel)

Lieutenant General Dan Shomron was arguably one of the most storied IDF officers and commanders. He served from 1987 to 1991 as the 13th Chief of Staff of the Israel Defence Forces, but was perhaps best known for his command of the 1976 raid on Entebbe, an operation in which the IDF launched a rescue in Uganda to free Israeli hostages held by the PLO after the hijacking of an El Al flight.

Per Israeli journalist Abraham Rabinovich, in his book *The Yom Kippur War*, each Egyptian division was armed with 73 Sagger missiles and 553 RPG rocket launchers, as well as 57 anti-tank guns and 90 recoilless guns. In addition to the 200 tanks attached to each division, this amounted to 800 or so individual anti-tank ordnances.

Egyptian infantrymen were vulnerable to artillery fire, but at that point, the Israelis had only about fifty artillery pieces along a 120km front that were themselves already under heavy counter-battery fire.

Despite the desperate battles underway, and the heavy losses already sustained, the picture that was returned to Sinai HQ, and onto the desk of General Gonan, was somewhat different to what was in fact taking place.

A rather seat-of-the-pants helicopter reconnaissance undertaken by Gonen's second-in-command returned what was regarded in the moment as a clear picture of the situation on the ground. This was that Israeli forces had reached the edge of canal, and had linked up with the various Bar Lev fortifications, leading to a sense at the command level that things were not quite as critical as they in fact were. There was, therefore, no particular urgency felt to order an evacuation of the frontline fortifications. This led to denials of permission to do so to small units who were fighting a series of desperate battles for survival.

An Israeli American-built M107 175mm self-propelled gun providing artillery support during the crossing of the Suez Canal. (Courtesy of GPO, Israel)

This undue complacency also affected central command, and the orders given by Elazar to Gonen during the early hours of Sunday morning tended to reflect this. Elazar authorised the evacuation of only those Bar Lev fortifications that were not critical to the defence of the canal, stressing that he did not want to place the emphasis on the defence of the line on these fortifications. He would rather hold on to strongpoints that would hinder the development of the enemy's main efforts. Such orders would have been met with absolute incredulity along the Bar Lev line at that moment, where the question had become one of mere survival.

Elazar emerges from the war, and the inevitable light of scrutiny that has since been played over all his actions as a credible commander under the most challenging conditions. In respect of the Clausewitzian pattern of central command, he realised that the moment-by-moment conduct of the war was beyond his control, and that it was the responsibility of his commanders on the ground. One must appreciate in this regard that, during this confused first day, he was concerned not only with events in the southern sector, but also to the north on the Golan Heights, were a similar fog of confusion hung over a battle that was no less bloody and desperate.

For the time being, Elazar's view of the southern sector was mollified by reports that he was receiving. He seemed overall to be satisfied that things were going well. Obviously the holding operation, now very much underway, would be a very difficult one, but he began to cast his mind ahead to Monday, the soonest that Israeli counter-attacks along the Suez could be expected to begin. The business at hand now was the mobilisation of reserves. Bearing in mind the operational depth available to the Israelis in the Sinai, which was not available on the Golan, his main effort was, for the time being at least, concentrated there.

If the situation along the Suez Canal was obscure, then the situation on the Golan Heights was even more so. The Golan Heights, a much-storied district of northern Israel, southern

Yom Kippur War. Israeli American-built M50 Sherman tanks prepare for a counter-attack on Syrian positions on the Golan Heights. (Courtesy of GPO, Israel)

Lebanon, northern Jordan and south-western Syria, had existed as a frontline of the Arab-Israeli conflict since its occupation by Israel in 1967. The landscape is one of relatively cool uplands, measuring roughly 50km by 30km, and lying at an average altitude of 1,000m. Hardly ideal tank country, the topography is rolling, with the gentler slopes mainly in its mid-section. It is characterised by a basalt surface, frequently scattered with boulders, and with larger outcrops that in many places inhibit the free movement of tracked vehicles. Vegetation is sparse, with some cultivation here and there, although essentially the region remains pastoral.

From the Syrian side it is more approachable in mass formation, while on its western edge, the escarpment falls away more steeply. At the south, the rugged Yarmuk Valley marks the border with Jordan, an effective barrier against the movement of mechanised forces or armour. Roughly from north to south run two roads. The Ceasefire Road and the TAP road, or Tapline Road, follow the underground Trans Arabian Pipeline (TAP) that originates in Saudi Arabia, and crosses the Golan en route to Lebanon. Five lateral roads cross from west to east, leading into Israel, with bridges spanning the River Jordan.

Confronting the Israelis along the Purple Line was a conventional force of three Syrian divisions – the 7th, 9th and 5th – each organised along Soviet lines, with a strong armoured brigade of around 200 tanks per division. Two additional armoured divisions were deployed to the rear – the 3rd and 1st – each with a strength of 250 tanks, and with the addition of a handful of independent brigades. This brought the total of Syrian tanks poised to assault the heights to approximately 1,500, supported by about 1,000 artillery pieces deployed in 600 units. These included the addition of heavy mortars and a series of SAM batteries – 150 in total, with 62 on the frontline, protecting the front line and Damascus, the Syrian capital, located no more than 50km east of the Purple Line. The Syrian tanks were, for the most part, of the Soviet

Yom Kippur War. The tail portion of a SAM-6 missile on the Golan Heights. (Courtesy of GPO, Israel)

Yom Kippur War. An Israeli A-4 Skyhawk providing infantry air cover moving into a forward battle-zone on the Golan Heights. (Courtesy of GPO, Israel)

T-62 pattern, the most modern on the battlefield, supported by a mechanised infantry of about 150,000 men, further supported by tanks, and including 800 or more armoured troop carriers.

Opposing this leviathan stood a comparatively miniature Israeli force, comprising two armoured brigades: the 7th in the northern sector and the 188th in the south, with a total strength of 170 tanks, and no more than 60 artillery pieces. These were US M60 Patton and British Centurion tanks, modified and modernised, but comparatively old in relation to those with which the Syrians were armed.

There were also various fortifications, better defended than those along the Suez Canal, but not of a significant weight. These were manned by a brigade of two infantry battalions and four batteries of artillery, each with six guns. Obstacles and mines protected the force, with the further addition of a 3m tank ditch dug almost along the entire ceasefire line. The tank battalions were positioned about 1,800m to the rear, supported by eleven batteries fielding large 155mm guns. Behind the lines, at a point called Nafekh Fort, surrounded by a large military encampment, was the Golan front HQ.

GOC of Northern Command was 46-year-old Major General Yitzak Hofi. Hofi's military pedigree, like most others of the high command during October 1973, was forged in 1948 and consolidated in 1967.

The Northern Sector HQ was moved from Nazareth to Nafekh on 5 October, a day before the outbreak.

Yom Kippur War. Long-range guns giving supporting fire to Israeli armour fighting on the Syrian Front. (Courtesy of GPO, Israel)

Yom Kippur War. Chief of Staff David Elazar, right, conferring with *Aluf* Yitzhak Hofi, left, and *Tat Aluf* (Brigadier General) Adam Yekutiel. (Courtesy of GPO, Israel)

Yom Kippur War. The Hermon Fortress (*Mutzav Ha- Hermon*) recaptured by Israeli troops. (Courtesy of GPO, Israel)

His signature contribution to the war of October 1973, however, and notwithstanding his credible command of the sector during the fighting, was made before the first shots were fired. His observations of the Syrian build-up along the Purple Line did not conform with the comforting assessments of his colleagues. He was insistent that more was at play than merely a display of posturing, or a defensive deployment. His was something of a lonely voice in the many security meetings and gatherings that preceded the war, warning that the Golan could be easily overrun if intelligence warnings failed, and if the understrength 188th Armoured Brigade was not reinforced. It was Hofi also, at least according to most accounts, who pointed to the heavy concentrations of SAM batteries in forward deployment, covering not only Syrian airspace, but the Golan too. This was a clear indication of Syrian ambitions to launch an operation in that theatre.

In the end, it was Dayan who partially responded to Hofi's concerns. During a visit to the Golan, he stood at an observation point and played his own binoculars over the Syrian deployments a few kilometres to the east, and agreed that reinforcements would be wise. He ordered a second armoured brigade, the 7th, currently concluding exercises in the Sinai, to move up to the Golan. Its last elements only arrived in theatre at noon on 6 October, two hours before the first shots were fired.

On the western slopes of Mount Hermon, at a height of about 2,000m, an Israeli observation point, perhaps the most important installation on the Golan, commanded a view over the entire battlefield. It was a strongly fortified position, but unfortunately incomplete at the commencement of the war, and defended by a force of only thirteen men.

The Syrian plan, something more of a blunt instrument than that of the Egyptians, was simply to punch a hole in Israeli defences and drive down to the east bank of the Jordan. In doing so they would not only recapture the Golan, but also place itself in a position to menace key Israeli population areas. This attack was to be spearheaded by three frontline

Yom Kippur War. One of the Israeli 175mm long-range guns firing at Syrian targets on the northern front. (Courtesy of GPO, Israel)

divisions, and supported by two reserve divisions. The assault would be general, focusing primarily along the line of the Tapline Road, and a gap in the broken country, the Rafid Gap, before plunging into the Israeli midriff and branching out to seize the Jordan valley. Based on the assumption that Israeli reserves would take at least twenty-four hours to be mobilised, the Syrians, with good reason, anticipated the conquest of the Golan Heights to the western escarpment in a single day. There were no operational plans thereafter to continue in any depth into Israel, but an advance on the Arab city of Nazareth was left open as a possibility.

At precisely 2.00pm on 6 October, about 100 Syrian aircraft hit targets across the Golan, while almost simultaneously, batteries of Syrian artillery began to lay down a creeping barrage to cover the advance of infantry and armour. As the first Syrian shells erupted, Israeli tank hatches dropped, and engines fired up. UN observers along the ceasefire line dived for cover, from where they observed the action unmolested, with a ringside seat for the most part at one of the last, great tank battles of the century.

The initial air and artillery assault lasted about fifty minutes, after which the Syrians began their advance along a broad front, led by mine-exploding-flail tanks and armoured bulldozers to fill in the tank ditches as they were encountered. SU-100 self-propelled guns were interspersed with tanks, alongside infantry travelling in armoured personnel carriers, armed with Sagger and Snapper anti-tank missiles, and RPG-7s.

Syrian airstrike targets did not include the Jordan bridges, upon the expectation that these might be required for a deeper penetration into Israel at a later point.

Within an hour or so the Syrians were over the ceasefire line, and quickly overrunning Israeli static positions. Israeli tanks supporting these emplacements retreated to prepared positions, and in broken ground in the hills overlooking the approaches, they and others began long-range sniping, registering hits from as far as 1,800m. This display of tank marksmanship caused the Syrians to later report that the Israelis were armed with speculative US-supplied laser fire-control.

One of the first Syrian targets was the observation post on the slopes of Mount Hermon, which was taken in a brief but bloody action by Syrian commandos. The sensitive electronic surveillance equipment that it had contained was sequestered by Soviet technicians, and quickly removed. This, without doubt, was a critical early loss for the Israelis, denying them a bird's-eye view of the battlefield, while a technical bonanza for the Soviets. An additional deployment of Syrian commandos on to the bridges of the Jordan, with the intention of inhibiting the Israeli crossing, was mooted, but never carried out.

As in the Sinai, the Israeli forward defence reeled under the shock and severity of the Syrian assault, being initially unclear to Hofi from which direction the Syrian main effort would be focused. The advance was on a broad front, but two main points of pressure quickly developed both north and south of the militarized zone. The Syrian 7th Infantry Division pressed past the Israeli occupied city of Quneitra, located on the north eastern edge of the Golan. The objective was to break through Israeli defences a few kilometres to the north of the city. This effort was stopped by the Israeli 7th Armoured Brigade, advantaged largely by good defensive positions and the movement of Syrian armour across open ground.

The Syrians withdrew within hours, leaving over sixty tanks destroyed or disabled in the field. At this stage, General Hofi suffered an agony of indecision as he attempted to determine in the confusion where to deploy his limited force. He sensed that the action around Quneitra was a feint, but he could not be certain. He therefore ordered the 7th Armoured Brigade,

Yom Kippur War. Israeli armour starting the breakthrough of the Syrian lines on the Golan Heights. (Courtesy of GPO, Israel)

Yom Kippur War. A Syrian T-62 tank with its turret blown off on the Golan Heights. (Courtesy of GPO, Israel)

under the command of Brigadier Rafael Eitan, to hold that sector, including the all-important Damascus Road (through Quneitra).

Farther south, however, at two strategic points – the Kudne and Rafid gaps – the main Syrian effort began to develop. Although bedevilled by bottlenecks and traffic jams, elements of the Syrian 5th Infantry Division broke through the Kudne Gap relatively easily, driving Israeli tanks ahead of it. Along the Tapline Road, two brigades of the Syrian 9th Infantry forced their way through the wide Rafid Gap, and began moving west.

Overhead, the IAF came briefly into action. Plunging directly into the Syrian air-defence barrier, however, it lost thirty aircraft within a few disastrous hours. The brunt of fighting, however, fell on the Israeli 188th Armoured Brigade, the celebrated 'Barak', or 'Lightning' Brigade. According to Chaim Herzog, the 188th was reduced to no more than fifteen operational tanks during those first few hours of fighting.

One of the most stirring acts of individual valour, recorded on a day often regarded as the darkest in Israeli military history, and filled with individual acts of bravery, was that mounted by a young tank commander by the name of Lieutenant Zvika Greengold. This episode has

On 7 October, Hofi ordered an operation to retake the observation post on the slopes of Mount Hermon. This was unsuccessful, and about twenty-two Israeli troops were killed and some fifty wounded in the effort.

One of Eitan's first orders was the evacuation of Quneitra.

An Israel Air Force Mirage with Rafael Shafrir II missiles on underwing hardpoints. (Courtesy of GPO, Israel)

since entered Israeli military legend, and might perhaps serve as an illustrative vignette of events as the evening of the first day drew in.

Greengold was unattached at the time, but, as was the case with numerous men hearing that the war had broken out, he hitchhiked to Nafekh where, at 9.00pm, he was given command of two repaired Centurion tanks. With these he was sent, without specific orders, down the Tapline Road towards the advancing Syrians. He soon contacted an advance section of the Syrian 51st Independent Tank Brigade. Engaging them, he destroyed six enemy tanks before his own was damaged. Exchanging it for the second tank in his detachment, he sent the damaged Centurion back, and continued the engagement, destroying or disabling a further ten Syrian tanks of the 452nd Tank Battalion in the gathering dusk. Confused into believing that this force of a single tank was at least a company, the Syrians withdrew.

For the next twenty hours or so, Greengold fought either alone or in combination with other improvised Israeli arrivals as they began to take to the field. As darkness fell, the Israeli defence along the Tapline Road degenerated into numerous, similarly desperate actions by improvised tank units, operating on a confused battlefield dominated by Syrian armour equipped with infrared night-fighting equipment. Greengold, yielding eventually to exhaustion, quit the battlefield with a personal claim of twenty tanks destroyed, although the popular estimate is closer to forty. For his performance that day, Lieutenant Zvika Greengold was awarded the Israeli Medal of Valour, the nation's highest order for courage. He has since resided in the august Israeli pantheon of war heroes.

It is worth noting that the only other Medal of Valour awarded on the Golan during this action was to a 29-year-old lieutenant colonel by the name of Avigdor Kahalani, who commanded the 77th Armoured Battalion during the action that came to be known as the *Emek HaBacha*, or the *Valley of Tears*. This episode, that played out between 6 and 9 October, saw, once again,

Above: Destroyed Syrian T-62 tanks and engineering equipment left behind by the retreating Syrian forces on the Golan Heights. (Courtesy of GPO, Israel)

Right: Israeli *Sgan Aluf* (Lieutenant Colonel) Avigdor Kahalani receiving the Medal of Valour for outstanding bravery in the battle on the Golan Heights during a ceremony at Beit Hanassi in Jerusalem. (Courtesy of GPO, Israel)

the desperate holding action of Israeli tank brigades against enormous odds. This time it was along the line of the northern assault where much of the force was concentrated, close to the ceasefire line in the northeast of the Heights, in a shallow valley that became a surreal graveyard of men and equipment, and was thereafter named the 'Vale', or 'Valley of Tears'.

As the sun rose on the second day, sixteen hours after the first assault, it was revealed that the Israeli forces had been driven back to the western edge of the Golan plateau. The Israeli 188th Armoured Brigade had been effectively annihilated.

By noon on the 7th, according to most accounts, ninety per cent of the brigade's officers had been killed, and it was fielding no more than a handful of serviceable tanks. According to Chaim Herzog, Syrian tanks were now poised just ten minutes' drive by tank from the east bank of the Jordan. A Syrian effort to take the fort at Nafekh was stopped in the middle of the camp, as brigade commander, General Rafael Eitan, slipped out under fire. Miraculously, however, the line held.

At dawn that morning, Moshe Dayan flew into Nafekh by helicopter, where he found General Hofi exhausted and demoralised. An already unnerved Dayan was shocked by what he saw. The Golan, he private concluded, might have to be abandoned. Lieutenant General Moshe Peled, at the head of a reserve armoured division that had by then begun to mobilise, was dismayed to be ordered by Hofi to deploy his tanks as they arrived along the Jordan River,

Six Medals of Valour were awarded for acts of conspicuous bravery during the various actions in the Sinai.

Yom Kippur War. Israeli troops moving in to counter-attack Syrian forces on the Golan Heights. (Courtesy of GPO, Israel)

76

implying an expectation that the Golan would be abandoned. General Haim Bar-Lev, former chief of staff now serving as troubleshooter for his successor, arrived a few hours after Dayan. He overrode Hofi's orders, ordering Peled instead to deploy his division from the south, pushing northwards in an effort to sever Syrian supply lines. By then reserves were beginning to arrive at the front in appreciable numbers. Although deployments were haphazard, the exhausted defenders of the night before were gradually relieved, and although still desperate, the situation began by degrees to stabilise.

In the south, as evening introduced a lull in the fighting, Egyptian engineers made good use of the hours of darkness to complete bridging operations. Thanks to their sectional design and easy repair, most of the Egyptian bridges held, despite the sporadic attentions over the course of the following day from the IAF. The movement of men and equipment across the canal continued, and was successfully completed by midday on the 7th. Thereafter, the Egyptian Second and Third armies began to organize and consolidate in preparation for the expected Israeli counter-attack. Assuming victory, the Egyptian strategy was then simply to reinforce their positions and widen the bridgeheads to a depth of between 6km and 8km.

And quite as anticipated, a rapid counter-attack was precisely what lay on the table in the Israeli command bunker in Tel Aviv. By then, the true cost of the previous day's fighting was beginning to be appreciated. After the novelty of a battlefield drubbing at the hand of the Arabs, it began to dawn on the Israeli high command that, in combination with the situation on the Golan, the IDF was hanging on by the skin of its proverbial teeth. Although the mobilisation of reserves had begun, a desperately thin line of Israeli tanks was all that was holding back an armed and equipped Egyptian expeditionary force.

Appeals for air support were continuing to come in from the beleaguered Bar Lev forts, a handful of which were still holding out. Although this was promised, dawn on 7 October saw IAF jets redirected north to deal with the even more perilous situation on the Golan. There, a lack of operational depth meant that a penetration of only a few kilometres would bring Syrian tanks into Israel. The south, despite its losses, and the sense of urgency felt by those fighting in that sector, could hold out longer.

An Israeli Air Force F-4 Phantom with a full load of ordnance. (Courtesy of GPO, Israel)

By then General Mandler was in a position to report the melancholy fact that, of the 290 Israeli tanks of his brigade that had gone into action the previous afternoon, less than a third remained operational. Without air support, and with the effective arrival of reserves still hours away, General Gonen saw no alternative but to withdraw the surviving Israeli tank units, and to order the evacuation of the Bar Lev fortifications where this was possible. Authorisation to this effect was requested from Tel Aviv, and soon afterwards given. At that point the mauled and humbled Israeli tank brigades disengaged, and began a slow but orderly withdrawal back across Artillery Road.

By this time, as reserve brigades began to arrive in the theatre, General Gonen consolidated and established a new order of battle, creating two new divisional commands. The northern sector was placed under the command of Major General Avraham Adan, and the southern sector retained by General Mandler, while a central division was created and placed under the command of Major General Ariel Sharon.

Sharon had by then already retired from a successful and high-profile career in the regular IDF in order to enter fulltime politics. He died in 2014, and although stalked by controversy throughout his career, he is nonetheless regarded by the Israelis as one of the greatest field commanders and professional soldiers ever produced by the IDF. His military career began with the creation of an independent Israeli military establishment, and his military pedigree can be traced back to the original 1948 war of Israeli independence. Part of the difficulty, and perhaps even the folly of Sharon's deployment as a reserve officer to the southern command sector, was the fact that he had himself held that command since 1969, relinquishing it only two months prior to the outbreak. General Gonen had, during that period, served under him, and therefore it was inevitable that Sharon, a man of considerable self-possession, should have bridled under the command of a perceived subordinate. Even before he left for the front, he clearly had a preconceived idea of how the campaign in the south would be won.

According to his military colleague and friend, Ze'ev Amit, as the two prepared to set off for the front, Amit posed the question, 'How are we going to get out of this?' to which Sharon replied, 'You don't know? We will cross the Suez Canal and the war will end over there.'

That evening, General Elazar arrived by helicopter at the Southern Command HQ and laid out his plans for a counter-attack scheduled for the following day. Notwithstanding its minutia, the plan was essentially a simple one. It conformed once again to the base Israeli doctrine of an armoured cavalry action without substantial air support, and with limited infantry support. From the north, a rolling armoured advance at divisional strength by General Adan's division would coincide with a push south by Mandler as far as Port Twefiq. This, under the circumstances, was a bold strategy, somewhat over-emphatic, and lacking perhaps in creativity. It was planned without the benefit of comprehensive reconnaissance, and upon an assumption of Egyptian deployments and order of battle.

However, in what might be regarded as a deliberate act, either of caution or command politics – perhaps both – Sharon's division, potentially the most aggressive, was held in reserve upon the contingency that, should Adan's assault fail, Sharon would form a supporting reserve. It was further mooted that a limited crossing into Egypt might be attempted. This latter contingency, however, was left vague, and might perhaps have been added simply to mollify Sharon who had already begun to aggressively assert his opinion

Right: Yom Kippur War. *Aluf* Arik Sharon, on the radio, in a mobile armoured command post in the Sinai Desert. (Courtesy of GPO, Israel)

Below: Yom Kippur War. *Aluf* Ariel Sharon shares a light moment with his troops on the west bank of the Suez Canal. (Courtesy of GPO, Israel)

Aluf Avraham Adan, Commander of the Israeli Armoured Corps. (Courtesy of GPO, Israel)

that a crossing of the canal to disrupt the Egyptian rear was the only way to quickly and comprehensively win the war.

The initial thrust of the counter-attack called for the northern division, under General Adan's command, to move south along the main lateral road, and then break up to brigade strength to assault the enemy at three strategic points along the canal, concentrating broadly around Ismailia and the Firdan Bridge.

The lack of prior reconnaissance proved telling soon after the advance began, as the division almost immediately found itself too far to the east, moving away from the main concentrations of Egyptian force. This, when recognised and corrected, left the Israelis moving *across* the Egyptian front, exposed to anti-tank action. The main attack then developed east to west, into positions that the Egyptians had prepared for precisely such an approach.

The first action, reported at about midday, saw a brigade enter Egyptian positions. In a replay of the day before, Egyptian tank-killer teams simply stepped out of their foxholes, appearing as if out of nowhere, unleashing a combination of missiles and rockets that quickly took twelve Israeli tanks out of commission. However, since the bulk of the division was moving too far to the east, the lack of immediate contact with the enemy convinced General Gonen, seated at the operations desk in the command bunker at Refidim, that all was going well. He therefore released Sharon's division to proceed south as a preliminary to the proposed assault against Egyptian Third Army positions. No sooner had Sharon mobilised, however, than distress calls began to come in to command HQ from the two brigades of Adan's division that had blundered into strong Egyptian defences. A major battle then ensued, with the Israelis surrounded on three sides by thousands of Egyptian infantry, and taking significant casualties. Gonen abruptly reversed his order to Sharon, instructing him now to move northwards in support of Adan's beleaguered brigades, but he was now too far south to practically accomplish this.

Thus, the Israeli counter-attack began to unravel. Sharon was enraged at the wastage of his potential through contradictory orders, and a fruitless series of back and forth manoeuvres that had achieved nothing. Adan was able to withdraw, albeit with heavy losses, but with the satisfaction at least of inflicting similarly heavy losses on the Egyptians. The inescapable result, however, was a failed counter-attack, and further unsustainable losses of Israeli men and equipment.

Only then did it seem to occur to Elazar, and the Israeli high command, that priority ought to be given to conservation of force, and the build-up of reserves. The events of that day, even more than on the first, brought into sharp focus critical flaws in Israeli tactical thinking ahead of the war. In both instances, the instinctive Israeli response had been an armoured cavalry charge in the face of entrenched Egyptians, by then brutally effective in anti-tank and tank-killer

Above: Yom Kippur War. *Aluf* Avraham Adan briefing Defence Minister Moshe Dayan. (Courtesy of GPO, Israel)

Right: War of Attrition. An Israeli M50 howitzer in the Suez Canal area: an M4 Sherman-tank-chassis-based, self-propelled artillery piece, mounting an Obusier Modèle 50 155mm L/30 howitzer in large enclosed superstructure area. (Courtesy of GPO, Israel)

The Firdan Bridge is a swing bridge that connects rail transit across the Suez Canal. It has been built and destroyed several times during the various phases of Arab-Israeli conflict, and in 1973 was decommissioned.

tactics. It would seem to represent a stultifying lack of creativity at a central command level, but also remarkable imperviousness to established armoured tactics that both attacks went in with neither preliminary reconnaissance nor infantry support, and without adequate artillery support.

It seems hardly surprising in the light of this that both attacks failed.

An additional factor of the disaster of 8 October was the ammunition that it gave Sharon to inflame an already tense command relationship between him and Gonen. While it is easy in hindsight to criticise, it is difficult to argue Sharon's position that a single, two-divisional assault, delivered against the lower quarter of the Second Army's bridgehead, would have successfully punched a hole in Egyptian lines, through which Israeli forces could either roll up the Egyptian Second Army's right flank, or cross the Suez into Egypt. Once on the west bank, Israeli forces could then effectively interdict Egyptian supply lines, isolate the Third Army and dismantle enough of the air-defence barrier to allow the IAF to operate. In the event, the Israelis lost a number of key positions and, with heavy losses, squandered an important opportunity. None of this could be denied, nor positively spun, and as the Israelis withdrew a sense of deep despondency settled on, not only the southern command, but the IDF establishment in general.

The following day, however, in a semi-official manoeuvre, Sharon launched an attack towards the canal. The move was ostensibly in an effort to retake a Bar Lev fortification that had fallen to the Egyptians the day before, but practically to explore the Egyptian defences in what was an armoured reconnaissance. Although ordered to break off the attack by Gonen, Sharon ignored the order, and probed with his forces into an abandoned canal-side agricultural project known as the Chinese Farm. Here the seam between the Egyptian Second and Third armies was discovered – the soft underbelly of the Egyptian Second Army. Recognising this immediately, Sharon withdrew, now armed with information that would prove vital in the days to come.

It was now decided to withdraw Israeli forces, to consolidate and to await the outcome of the battle raging on the Golan Heights. The military priority was now this sector, so for the time being forces in the Sinai were to be held back. With just 400 Israeli tanks surviving in the Sinai, Israel could ill afford to wage two major and simultaneous offensives, so Gonen was instructed simply to hold firm and avoid the temptation to engage.

Reorganisation and conservation were, for the time being, the key priorities. There was also, quite naturally, a great deal of concern now about mounting casualties, and the wastage of equipment and manpower that had so far been the principal outcome of Israeli action in the Sinai.

This was perhaps the darkest moment of the war for the Israelis. On both fronts, losses had been astronomical. In the south, tactical failures might have accounted for some part of this, but in the north it was a simple question of raw survival. Here, the thin line of Israeli defence was being relentlessly battered over the limited scope of a small field of battle by an enemy vastly superior in numbers. In the absence of a coherent strategy, Israeli units simply held on, and against a backdrop of extraordinary human heroism, and the superhuman efforts of individual commanders and tank crews, the line did indeed hold.

Right: A Shafrir air-to-air interception missile under the wing of an Israeli Mirage fighter. (Courtesy of GPO, Israel)

Below: Yom Kippur War. An Israeli convoy of reinforcements moving up towards the frontlines on the Golan Heights. (Courtesy of GPO, Israel)

8. THE POLITICS OF WAR, AND THE WAR OF POLITICS

This is the end of the Third Temple.

(Moshe Dayan)

It goes without saying that the Arab reactions to the initial successes of the 6 October war were jubilant, quite as a sense of deep shock and despondency settled on the Israelis.

The edifice of automatic Israeli military superiority had been ground to dust under the unexpected hammer and anvil of Israel's Arab neighbours. For six years, the expectation had been that, when this day came, a short war would produce another resounding Israeli victory. Instead, Israelis were exposed to the humiliating news reportage of downed Israeli pilots paraded before Arab television, Israeli prisoners of war squatting in the desert with their hands on their heads, and exaggerated reports of a situation that scarcely required exaggeration.

Defence Minister Moshe Dayan at the Northern Command. (Courtesy of GPO, Israel)

On the evening of 6 October, Israeli Prime Minister Golda Meir addressed the nation in a television broadcast that was upbeat and bullish, announcing that the Arabs had launched a war, but that Israeli forces were responding. Dayan followed a few hours later with his own address, which was no less upbeat. During the opening phases of the war, Israeli censorship had insulated the bulk of the population from the worst of the news. By degrees, however, the truth became known, by which time a sense of deep gloom pervaded the corridors of power, and even more so the command bunker in Tel Aviv.

As defence minister, Moshe Dayan was concerned more with defence policy than battlefield strategy, and throughout the war he deferred always to his chief of staff. Nonetheless, he has tended to emerge from the many accounts of the war as an agent of pessimism.

At first light on Sunday morning, as the first shock of Israeli losses during the last sixteen hours were being felt, Dayan flew by helicopter first to the northern front, where he encountered the demoralised Hofi. Then

84

later in the morning he left for Southern Command, at which point the unfounded optimism of the first few hours of the war was obliterated by the facts on the ground. Dayan, of course, had been one of the chief architects of post-1967 Israeli defence policy, which now lay in ruins in the graveyards of smoking tanks. He was concerned at the apparently unfounded optimism of General Gonen, then planning his first counter-attack, for there was nothing about the situation that inspired optimism in him.

Far from taking the fight to the enemy, Dayan advised Gonen that the priority now must surely be to establish a fall-back line that could be held if the current front crumbled. Abandon the Bar Lev forts, he advised, since too much energy and resource had been squandered attempting to break through. Reminding Gonen that he had the authority to order such a withdrawal should it be necessary, he concluded the meeting with the softer suggestion that Gonen consult with Elazar on the matter of a tactical withdrawal.

En route back to Tel Aviv, one can easily imagine that Dayan reflected on the disaster that had been his own strategic thinking, and how he, along with the entire Israeli defence establishment, had so underestimated the capabilities of the Arabs. The situation was indeed critical. In the words of Abraham Rabinovich, author of perhaps the most comprehensive account of the war: 'He [Dayan] was now probably the most depressed man in the country, certainly the most depressing.'

An Israeli Chaparral anti-aircraft missile system, with four missiles ready for launching from the retractable turret, having a 360 degree traverse and 90 degree elevation. (Courtesy of GPO, Israel)

Meeting first with Elazar, Dayan shared his apocalyptic vision and his doubts that Israel possessed the capacity in manpower and equipment to sustain the current effort. He reiterated to Elazar what he had already suggested to Gonen –a fall-back line in the Sinai, perhaps as far to the rear as the Sinai passes, and the abandonment of the Bar Lev fortifications. Elazar did not appear to share Dayan's sense of hopelessness, but spoke instead to his operational suggestion, agreeing that efforts to break through to the forts were at that moment pointless. Also. a second line of defence be established to the rear, but on the Lateral Road, where Sharon's and Adan's divisions were already in position.

The point, however, is less what was tactically decided, but more Dayan's sense – perhaps for the first time in his career – that Israel was not just facing two determined foes on two fronts. The nation was now facing the entire Arab world, the disunity of which was all that stood between Israel and a mighty coalition of forces that could destroy the young nation with terrifying ease.

After meeting with Elazar, he met the prime minister, Golda Meir, and to her he spoke in prophetic terms, using words that have since become iconic. 'This,' he said, 'is the end of the Third Temple.'

The ancient history of the Jews had seen the first temple of Jerusalem destroyed by the Babylonians in 586BC, and the second by the Romans in AD70. Now, the temple, rebuilt in 1948, was set to fall once again. Golda Meir would later recall that, at that moment, she contemplated suicide. To her personal assistant, whom she met in the corridor when stepping out to compose herself, she remarked that Dayan was contemplating surrender. After a cigarette, however, Meir composed herself, and ordered that the Israeli ambassador to the United States, Simcha Dinitz, be contacted. It was time, she announced, to begin applying pressure on Washington.

Dinitz was a man well known to Meir. Prior to his appointment as Israeli ambassador to the United States, he had served as director general of the prime minister's office, and as such he had been her key adviser since her election in 1969. He was, on the surface, a quiet and unprepossessing man, but he was a patriot and a determined diplomat. Although respectful of Kissinger, he was not by any means overawed by him.

On Monday, 7 October, at that point in the war when the Israeli leadership was drawing optimistic conclusions, Dinitz met Kissinger, delivering to him a similarly upbeat report. This segued well into Kissinger's own view of the battlefield. His diplomatic handling of the situation thus far had tended to be informed by the majority opinion that Arab aggression would be rewarded by an early defeat. There were, however, one or two political nuances that seemed to have escaped him, which was perhaps because he did not immediately appreciate the implications of Egypt's subtle shift of foreign policy. It was not lost on him, however, that in one way or another, the conclusion of this current outbreak of war in the Middle East would lead to a peace process.

Sadat's unyielding demand for a total Israeli withdrawal from the occupied territories was an opening position, because it was too improbable to be otherwise. He had not, however, read Sadat's controversial expulsion of Soviet advisers as an invitation to the US to engage more closely – at least not immediately. Neither had he contemplated the rationale of starting an unwinnable war simply to regain Arab self-respect, and certainly, nor had he given any particular thought to the possibility that Israel might be defeated.

The ebb and flow of the Soviet position as the days passed is also interesting. The expulsion of Soviet advisers and the general disregard for Soviet advice to avoid open war had tended

An armed F-4 Phantom of the Israeli Air Force. (Courtesy of GPO, Israel)

to ferment a sense in the Kremlin that the Egyptians were shortly to get what was coming to them. There was a willingness, therefore, to sit back and watch matters unfold, after which the Soviets expected to assume a 'we told you so' posture, after which Soviet diplomatic reconstruction would again place Moscow on the centre stage. Lacking perhaps Kissinger's nose for diplomatic subtlety, the underlying point of Sadat's launching an unwinnable war was less obvious in the Kremlin than in Washington.

President Assad, at least according to some sources, had laid the groundwork in the days prior to the launch of the war by gaining assurances from the Soviets that a ceasefire would be sought forty-eight hours into the war in order to lock in Arab territorial gains. However, when, within forty-eight hours, the Soviet ambassador to Cairo broached that matter with Sadat, he was angrily rebuffed. Then, as the predicted Arab collapse played out – initially at least as a stunning Arab *tour de force* – the Soviets were somewhat thrown on the back foot.

Kissinger, in the meanwhile, having heard Dinitz's initial assessment of the war, was rather surprised a day lay later to be woken in the early hours of the morning, just twenty-four hours later, by an anguished telephone call from Dinitz, requesting the ramping up of US arms shipments to Israel. Somewhat irritated, Kissinger told Dinitz that it could be discussed in the morning. Dinitz relayed this back to Meir, who retorted that tomorrow might be too late. She ordered her ambassador to telephone Kissinger again, which he did. This caused Kissinger to reflect that, unless the Israeli ambassador was trying to prove to the Israeli cabinet that he could pull the US secretary of state out of bed at will, something very serious was afoot. A few hours later, Kissinger, Dinitz and a handful of State Department aides met in the map room of the Whitehouse. At this point the degree of Israel's predicament began to sink in.

Israeli American-made M109, 155mm self-propelled howitzers in the Sinai. (Courtesy of GPO, Israel)

Around 50 warplanes and 500 tanks – 400 in the Sinai alone – had been eaten up in initial operations. Kissinger was stunned. How did this happen? Dinitz shrugged his shoulders. He had no idea, but it certainly went some way to explaining Sadat's current attitude. Towards the end of the meeting Golda Meir put through a telephone call to Washington. Through Dinitz, she appealed for an opportunity to visit the US to plead directly with Nixon on her own behalf. Obviously she meant business, but no less obviously a visit by the Israeli prime minister at this juncture would be impossible. It would not only be a sign of panic, but it would bring any potential arms resupply to Israel out in the open, and as such compromise the future role of the United States as mediator in the peace process. Kissinger demurred, but with the assurance that he would do what he could.

Later in the day, Kissinger met top administration officials, where he encountered a sceptical front over the question of Israel's immediate peril. US support would only be relevant to ensure Israel's survival, not to assist her in smashing the Arabs. Kissinger's argument – the same argument as would begin to dawn on the Soviets – was that a defeat of American arms by Soviet arms would be a geopolitical disaster. The US now had no choice but to resupply the IDF before it was too late. Nixon, then embroiled in Watergate, and no doubt welcoming a diversion, agreed, instructing Kissinger to inform the Israelis that their arms requirements would be met.

At this juncture, in Tel Aviv the question of the deployment of nuclear weapons came under discussion. Dayan's 'Third Temple' prognostications, and a sense of panic at the heart of the military command, had opened the possibility of the unthinkable.

By Tuesday morning, news of the failure of the Sinai counter-attack the day before had been digested, and as the chiefs of staff pondered almost unbelievable equipment and manpower losses, a general sense that the nation's back was against the wall pervaded the bunker.

An Israeli Air Force F-4 Phantom. (Courtesy of GPO, Israel)

Commander of the Israeli Armoured Corps, *Aluf* Israel Tal, demonstrating one of the new armoured vehicles to previous chiefs of staff in the presence of Yitzhak Rabin during their visit to the army. (Courtesy of GPO, Israel)

In the words of General Israel Tal, sometime commander at the southern front: 'We didn't have any reserves left, there was nothing left. The war was perceived not just at a critical, almost hopeless stage, but as a struggle for our very physical survival.'

It was more or less then, according to a 2003 book published by Israeli investigative journalist, Ronen Bergman, entitled *Yom Kippur – The Moment of Truth*, that senior Israeli military leaders first mooted the idea of deploying Israel's nuclear weapons to avert what was increasingly appearing to be the eve of Israel's destruction. It was Dayan, perhaps the most visibly shaken by events of all his cabinet colleagues, who suggested the possibility to Golda Meir. No detailed record has so far surfaced of what was said at this meeting, but he clearly stated and believed that Israel was fast approaching a moment of profound decision. Here, however, opinions vary considerably on the degree of decision made by the Israelis over the question of nuclear weapons.

According to Edgar O'Ballance, already cited earlier, Golda Meir gave her permission for their preparation on Wednesday, 9 October. According to Ronen Bergman, on the other hand, Meir refused, opting instead to increase pressure on the US for immediate resupply.

In a 2003 *New York Times* interview with Naftali Lavie, Moshe Dayan's spokesman during the war, Dayan was himself committed to the use of nuclear weapons. Abraham Rabinovich, another notable historian, who researched and chronicled the war as it was being fought, reported the comments of Professor Yuval Ne'eman. A nuclear physicist and Israeli intelligence official, the professor admitted that, although nuclear capable missiles were prepared and deployed, the question of their warheads was left open for general interpretation, and the decision to employ them was never made.

Nonetheless, that the discussion came up at all is a clear indication of the closeness to which the Israeli political and military leadership felt the proximity of defeat. Clearly, in those critical hours, the question was simply one of Israel's basic survival. Whatever might have been the truth, it is very probable that the open discussion of nuclear deployment, in coded but easily understandable language, was intended at the very least to crystallise in the minds of senior US leaders as to how serious this situation was, and how serious were the Israelis. A nuclear confrontation in a relatively minor Cold War theatre held the potential for a superpower escalation, and this was certainly something to be avoided.

In Cairo, Sadat had begun to receive visits from the diplomatic representatives of several Arab and Western countries, including Britain and the Soviet Union. The messages delivered in general probed the possibility of a ceasefire, but after months of meticulous caution, Sadat finally succumbed to hubris, and angrily eschewed any such discussion. He was in constant touch with his military chiefs, and was monitoring the progress of the war very carefully. Its smooth prosecution so far had, quite frankly, amazed him. He was now inclined to wonder how much further the envelope might be pushed.

Nonetheless, he was cautious too. The strategy agreed between he and Assad had included the understanding, upon a successful crossing of the Suez Canal, of a quick Egyptian push inland to seize the Sinai passes. This was key to the Syrian strategy, simply because the engagement of a large force of IDF on the borders with Egypt would naturally limit the numbers of men and resources available to fight on the Golan. As Egyptian forces in the Sinai established their bridgeheads and dug in, and as the battle for the Golan raged, Syrian queries began to be heard regarding the commencement of phase two, about which nothing was heard from Cairo. It was indeed at this point, on or about 9 and 10 October, that the Syrian advance on the Golan was broken, and began very slowly to be turned back.

Yom Kippur War. Israeli half-tracks covered by a self-propelled gun, move troop reinforcements up to the Golan Heights. (Courtesy of GPO, Israel)

The turning point for the Israelis, however, came with the establishment of a steady resupply of equipment from the United States, along with the effective deployment of its reserves. The battles on both fronts of 8 and 9 October, and the balance of strength on 10 October, gave way to a rapid Syrian reversal, beginning, more or less, on the 11 October.

The US resupply operation was a tacitly understood fact, and it was agreed that, if Israel could deal with the logistics of transport, supplies would be made available. Almost the entire El Al fleet, with numbers painted out, diverted to the transport of US arms and supplies.

The most urgent requirements were the latest electronic countermeasure (ECM) pods to counteract the latest SAMs, but the urgent replacements of aircraft and tanks could not be handled by a civilian carrier. Pressure therefore remained on the US to ramp up the movement of supplies through its own military transport capacity.

Kissinger was obviously reluctant to authorise an official operation to bail out the Israelis, bearing in mind that there were wider foreign policy implications than just that of Israel's survival. The British, for example, had declared an arms embargo against the Israelis, as had the French, and there was little international appetite to sanction, aid or assist an American airlift. There was also the question of the likely Soviet response to an overt US airlift. On 10 October, though, this concern was somewhat neutralised when, having reviewed recent satellite imagery, and sobered by what they saw, the Soviets began their own arms shipments to relieve Syria and Egypt.

The US could quite easily then have done likewise, but Kissinger dragged his feet. As the Israelis were being beaten onto the ropes, he prevaricated, concerned about US relations with

Syrian soldiers hold their hands up in surrender on the Golan Heights during the Yom Kippur War (Courtesy of GPO, Israel)

The British arms embargo was a severe blow to the Israelis thanks to their reliance on British Centurion tanks.

A sealift was considered, of course, but rejected because of the urgency of Israeli requirements.

Operation Nickel Grass would conclude a month later, on 14 November 1973.

other Arab states, threats of an oil embargo and, of course, détente. He would later blame the US Department of Defence for the delay, but once aware of the extent of the Soviet airlift, he sought to source private charter aircraft to undertake the task.

No doubt, both the Department of Defence and the State Department had a hand in the delays, but in the end, it was a personal appeal to President Nixon from Prime Minister Golda Meir that triggered the operation. On 13 October, the US Air Force was ordered to undertake the airlift. Notwithstanding difficulties related to refuelling and flyover restrictions, Operation Nickel Grass swung into action and the Israel's lifeline began to flow.

The following day, the first US Lockheed C-5 Galaxy heavy-transport aircraft landed at Lod International Airport in Tel Aviv, carrying an assortment of weaponry, including the ADM-62 Walleye, a 'television- guided' bomb, and the CBU-100 Rockeye, a conventional, free-fall cluster bomb for use against small groups of infantry, tanks, guns or vehicles.

Above: Yom Kippur War. An IDF M107 175mm self-propelled gun shells Syrian targets from the northern Golan Heights. (Courtesy of GPO, Israel)

Right: Israeli American-built Raytheon MIM-23 Hawk ('Homing All the Way Killer') on a mobile-firing platform. (Courtesy of GPO, Israel)

A majority of NATO members, with the reluctant exception of Portugal, withheld permission for the overfly, landing or refuelling of US aircraft on their territories. All were wary of the threatened Arab oil embargo, and in some cases were pro-Arab, or at least anti-Israeli, as was the case with France. This forced the US to fly fighter jets directly from the US to Israel using USAF pilots, refuelling first over the mid-Atlantic using aerial tankers, and again over the Mediterranean. Heavier armaments, including tanks, helicopters, anti-tank missiles, ammunition and spares were sourced from NATO stockpiles. As all of this began to arrive, it was quickly absorbed, and most historians have tended to agree that there was not a moment to spare. The Israelis were critically short of ammunition and missiles of all types, as well as tanks and aircraft, various infantry vehicles and miscellaneous spare parts.

Kissinger, having pulled Israel back from the brink, now began exploring options for peace, calling initially for a ceasefire based on a return to positions held on 6 October, leaving Israel with all of the occupied territories. This suggestion, however, not only fell short of a United Nations proposal, but was immediately undermined by both a tightening of an OPEC oil embargo and the solidarity of the Arab world.

He then suggested that Syrian losses on the Golan be balanced out by Egyptian gains in the Sinai. By then, however, the lustre of IDF invincibility had lost a little of its gloss, leaving Kissinger no longer quite so confident as he had been that Israeli could lever the Egyptians out of the Sinai, even if they had the freedom to do so.

By now, on the battlefield the Israelis were quicker to absorb US materiel than the Arabs were to absorb Soviet supplies. With the steady arrival and organisation of reserves on the frontlines, the military stalemate of 9 and 10 October began to tell in favour of the Israelis. This will be dealt with in more detail in the next chapter, but for the moment, the political effect of this was manifest in increased superpower posturing.

US intelligence reports suggested that the Soviets were shipping nuclear warheads to Egypt for use in SCUD missiles. Soon afterwards, the US 6th Fleet put in an appearance in the eastern Mediterranean, shadowed soon afterwards by the Soviet Mediterranean Squadron. For several weeks afterwards, the two fleets circled one another at sea.

The Soviet squadron had fifty-two vessels of various classes, while the 6th Fleet initially had forty-eight, including two carriers – the USS *Independence*, then in port in Greece, and the USS *Franklin D. Roosevelt* in Spain.

The energy crisis of this period was somewhat coincidental to the hostilities underway in the Middle East, and the threat of an oil embargo for the most part remained only that. Saudi Arabia, the main oil exporter in the region, and a firm political ally of the USA, was nonetheless disappointed when the USA did not respond to Sadat's 1972 expulsion of Soviets from Egypt by in turn applying pressure on Israel to negotiate over the occupied territories. The uncompromising US support for 'Zionist' Israel did not, for the most part, endear it to the Arab states. Direct Arab pressure, in terms of price rises and embargoes, did not begin to occur – or be felt – until after the ceasefire, and perhaps influenced subsequent diplomatic manoeuvres more than they did military ones.

Defence Minister Moshe Dayan inspecting a knocked-out Syrian tank near Quneitra on the Golan Heights. (Courtesy of GPO, Israel)

Both fleets bristled at one another, with occasional warnings traded. Both admirals – Daniel Murphy and Yevgeni Volubuyev – in later private assessments acknowledged a very high likelihood of one fleet attacking the other, leading to a very high likelihood thereafter of mutual destruction.

A week later, the Egyptian Third Army was now surrounded in the Sinai Desert, and the military situation had almost entirely reversed in favour of the Israelis. Responding to pleas from Cairo, Soviet leader Leonid Brezhnev warned Washington that if Israel did not lift its siege of the Third Army, the Soviet Union would have to consider sending in troops to do so. Soviet airborne divisions were placed on alert, and Admiral Volubuyev was ordered to organise a naval infantry force made up of volunteers from his squadron to be landed in Port Said at the mouth of the Suez Canal, in a show of Soviet support for Egypt.

The Pentagon's response was a worldwide alert – Defcon 3 (Defensive Condition), the highest state of readiness in peacetime. An American airborne division was placed on standby for immediate departure to the Middle East. Fifty B-52 strategic bombers were recalled from Guam to the US. A third carrier task force was ordered into the Mediterranean, and a 2,000-man Marine detachment with the 6th Fleet was moved south of Crete, closer to the battle area. The Soviet squadron, reinforced through the Dardanelles, now numbered ninety-seven vessels, including twenty-three submarines, while the 6th Fleet had expanded to sixty.

The stakes were now extremely high, and for each side the potential existed, if the opposing side won the standoff, that an opposing proxy would win the war. This would in turn influence

Yom Kippur War. Prime Minister Golda Meir, Defence Minister Moshe Dayan and Minister Israel Galili visiting the Southern Command in the Sinai. (Courtesy of GPO, Israel)

which side exercised greater control over the subsequent peace process, which would further affect the adjustment of superpower spheres of influence in the Middle East.

In the end, the two sides pulled back, with Moscow perhaps pulling back first and farthest. The Soviet desire to preserve détente was perhaps stronger, and no doubt, both sides stared down the prospect of mutually assured destruction with a very limited appetite. Through convoluted diplomatic channels, Moscow let it be known that its preference was for a UN-sponsored ceasefire. This won Washington's approval, after which tensions rapidly deescalated.

With the word 'ceasefire' now on the table, it became only a matter of time before a ceasefire would be negotiated and put into effect. Dinitz, when he met Kissinger again, did so representing a nation in somewhat less of a panic than it had been a day or two earlier. Discussions between the two ended with an undertaking from Kissinger that he would do what he could to delay a ceasefire resolution in the UN Security Council so that the Israelis could regain as much lost ground as possible. By then Israeli security talk was quite openly discussing a crossing of Israeli forces into Egypt, but before that could take place, there were battles yet to be fought.

9. THE TURNING OF THE TIDE

> Every IDF commander was deeply imbued with the idea that we would have to cross at some point. This was an organic part of the IDF's doctrine of transferring the war to enemy territory and terminating it there quickly.
>
> (Major General Avraham Adan)

The situation in the Sinai began to stabilise on 9 October, as the arrival of Israeli reserve units steadily fortified frontline positions, and as the Israeli field command began to get the measure of the battlefield. Resupply was taking place, and tactics were adapting from the initial cavalry assaults, so wasteful of Israeli armour, to a holding position against which Arab probing attacks exhausted themselves. Israeli tank crews also began to react to Arab anti-tank tactics with somewhat more positive results. Although General Ariel Sharon, the brilliant but compulsive division commander, agitated against the orders of Gonen to retain a static position, arguing for an immediate crossing into Egypt, the Israeli holding strategy held. It is perhaps worth noting that, after the costly battles of the evening of 6 October, and the failed counter-attack of 8 October, General Gonen was effectively relieved of his command by General Chaim Bar Lev. The potentially negative affect of a reshuffle at the command level was softened by Bar Lev's mandate as personal representative of the chief of staff, which did not technically usurp Gonen as GOC of Southern Command. This effected a supervisory role that in practical terms gave Bar Lev overall command. One of the first recommendations that Bar Lev made was for the removal of General Ariel Sharon from the theatre. This repeated proposal was rejected by Dayan because he feared that it would create unnecessary instability on the line. Sharon was as loved by his men as he was despised by his superiors, but also, no doubt, against wider, political considerations related to Sharon's rise in the political establishment.

It was understood now and acknowledged, that no final resolution to the campaign would occur while the IDF was bogged down in a static, attritional war that was traditionally favoured by the Arabs. The IDF was configured for mobility and action, and the only possible expression of that tactic was a crossing into Egypt that would take the action to the enemy. It was this that General Ariel Sharon favoured. Both Bar Lev and Gonen, and indeed Elazar himself, however, although recognising the logic, and perhaps the medium-term advantage of such a tactic, were

---

8 October 1967 is generally regarded as the lowest point in the short history of the IDF, and for this General Gonen shoulders significant blame. His overall command and offensive strategy was regarded then as it continues to be, as flawed, and lacking in creativity. Gonen was criticised severely by the Agranat Commission.

General Chaim, or Haim Bar Lev was another of Israel's military legends, his career forged in 1948, and consecutively honed in 1956 and 1967. He had himself served as GOC of Southern Command, and it was after him that the Bar Lev line was named.

Yom Kippur War. Chief of Staff David Elazar, on the left, speaking with *Aluf* Arik Sharon. (Courtesy of GPO, Israel)

mindful of the fact that two Egyptian reserve divisions remained deployed on the west bank of the Suez. Until they were committed to the war on the east bank, they posed too great a threat to an isolated Israeli expeditionary force separated by the canal, and at the end of a long supply line. It was clear that these two Egyptian reserve divisions, comprising two independent brigades and around 900 tanks, were intended to support an Egyptian break-out from their bridgeheads. It was therefore decided to delay any offensive action until, on the one hand, matters had been stabilised on the northern front, and the Egyptian reserve had been committed to the east bank on the other.

This was indeed the Egyptian intention, or to least the paper strategy that had been agreed to between Sadat and Assad, and upon which the Syrians had based their substantive tactical approach to the war. As the situation began to stabilise on the Golan, a great deal of diplomatic verbiage was exchanged between Damascus and Cairo, seeking clarification of this, while urging the Egyptians to act.

Sadat, extremely pleased with the performance of the Egyptian expeditionary force, and still firmly wedded to the concept of holding territory in the Sinai as a political bargaining chip, firmly resisted pressure from various sources to exploit this favourable tactical position by a further and rapid advance inland. His objective remained political, and he ordered, therefore, an operational pause. In this position, he enjoyed the support of his chief of staff, Lieutenant General Saad el Shazly, who was closer to the action on the battlefield, and could better appreciate matters for what they were. The IDF had been delivered a severe body blow, which had knocked it briefly back on the ropes, but the military imbalance between the two countries remained a factor. To act in haste upon the hubris of an early victory and by throwing the Egyptian divisions into an advance beyond their anti-aircraft shield would be madness.

> Readers will recall that this advance was order by General Bar Lev, overriding General Hofi's despairing orders to deploy the 146th along the Jordan as a preliminary to abandoning the Golan Heights.

On the afternoon of 8 October, General Shazly toured the front, visiting each divisional HQ, and from both, the same concerns were expressed. IAF damage to the heavy bridges that had facilitated the crossing of the armoured divisions had reduced their number to just one per division, raising the possibility of an interruption in supply and reinforcement. In each instance, the suggestion of the divisional commanders was for an operational pause to consolidate the bridgeheads and reorganise forces before the contemplation of any further offensive operations. Shazly agreed, and thus he resisted pressure to move.

Likewise, in Israel a sense prevailed that the position in the Sinai was not yet ripe for offensive action. Elazar appeared at Southern Command just after midnight on 9 October, and there he and Dayan met senior commanders to assess the military situation. It was agreed after this meeting that, with just 400 tanks remaining operational in the Sinai, Israel could hardly afford to wage two major offensives on two separate fronts. Elazar instructed his subordinates to avoid any major contacts, and to concentrate for the time being on consolidation and reorganisation. The counter-crossing of the Suez could wait. Matters on the northern front were now demanding their full attention, and all the forces and reserves that the IDF could muster.

By the end of 9 October – on day three of the war – General Yitzak Hofi, still in command of the northern sector, was thinking positively again. The 8th and 9th of October had been pivotal days. The initial impact of the Syrian assault, stopped at the very edge of the western escarpment, was checked on 7 October by the narrowest of margins. It was then pushed back during 8 October by the reserve Israeli 146th Division, led by Lieutenant General Moshe Peled. Peled advanced on the Syrian border from the south, moving north-east along the Israeli Route 98, retaking a number of forward IDF posts and liberating a handful of besieged Israeli troops. Farther north, the Syrian 9th Division renewed its effort to take control of the city of Quneitra, but came up against a reinforced Israeli 7th Brigade. A ferocious, close-quarter tank battle ensued, the last of the sequence of what would be known as the 'Valley of Tears'.

Syrian forces were pushed back from Nafekh Fort HQ, and by the end of the day, the bulk of Syrian forces in the occupied Golan had either been destroyed, or were moving back into Syria.

That night, at 10.00pm, an upbeat general staff meeting was held in Tel Aviv, during which the question under discussion was not if an Israeli counter-offensive on the Golan could succeed, but how far into Syria it would push. The Golan Heights offered no room for manoeuvre, and therefore no compromise over its re-occupation could be entertained. After Syrian forces had been removed from the Heights, a strategic demolition of the Syrian army, to the extent that that was possible, would be undertaken by the IDF to ensure the diminution, and, if possible, the removal of any future Syrian threat against Israel. This type of thinking was backed up by a renewed confidence in US logistical support and the concurrent mobilisation of the full diplomatic weight of the US behind Israel. Israel now had room to manoeuvre. The worst of it was over, and although a tough fight still lay ahead, the question now was simply whether to halt an advance at the Purple Line, or to drive the counter-offensive all the way to Damascus.

Yom Kippur War. Israeli troops move along the Quneitra–Damascus road on the Syrian Front. (Courtesy of GPO, Israel)

Yom Kippur War. Victorious Israeli troops on the road to the Syrian capital, Damascus. (Courtesy of GPO, Israel)

The issues to be considered were at what point, if at all, an Israeli advance into Syria would trigger Soviet intervention, as well as the actual intervention pending by neighbouring Arab states, particularly Iraq, from where news was already coming in of the movement of troops and armour to Syria. It was agreed, in consultation with the Israeli cabinet, to press the war into Syria, but not all the way to Damascus, which lay only 50km to the north-east of northern Golan. Elazar advocated the establishment of a line 15km in depth into Syria, which would neutralise the Syrian threat, place Damascus under IDF artillery range, and probably amplify Syrian pressure against Egypt to launch an attack in the south.

The commencement of the Israeli counter-offensive was planned for the morning of 11 October, five days into the war. General Yitzak Hofi, commanding the northern sector, settled on a concentrated assault across open country delivered from the north, with the massifs of Mount Hermon covering the left flank of the Israeli advance. Israeli divisions would attack westwards along the Israeli 91, 98 and 99 highways, the principal trunk roads linking Israel with Syria, and all leading by the shortest route to Damascus. Divisions led by Brigadier General Raphael Eitan and Major General Dan Laner respectively, would lead the attack. The reserve would be the 146th Division, part of Major General Laner's command and led by Lieutenant General Moshe Peled.

The 10th of October was spent in feverish preparation. Tanks were repaired, units replenished and recently supplied equipment and ammunition absorbed. The three divisions were cobbled together from units that had already seen significant action. According to Chaim Herzog, the 188th Tank Brigade, the battle-scarred and much-storied 'Barak', was operational

An Israeli tank crew parades in front of Centurion tanks in the Negev, only the NCO not armed with the ubiquitous Israeli 9mm Uzi sub-machine gun. (Courtesy of GPO, Israel)

with only one original company 2IC, and two platoon commanders. Not a single company commander survived the initial actions, and ninety per cent of the original command element had either been killed or wounded.

At 11.00am on 11 October, the 188th led the 7th into Syria, and almost immediately the game was on again.

Syrian forces, having retreated across the Purple Line in good order, had dug in, preparing for the inevitable. Waiting for the Israelis was a Moroccan expeditionary force, supported by forty tanks, itself supported by a Syrian infantry brigade armed with anti-tank ordnance and backed up by around thirty-five tanks. These forces blocked the road to the Syrian village of Mazraat Beit Jinn, astride the heavily fortified northern access route to Damascus. Fighting erupted almost at the moment that the Israelis came into range, and a heavy action was fought during the course of the afternoon. The engagement eventually saw the Israelis seizing a defended ridge of high ground, and securing the important crossroads just west of the Syrian village of Hader.

The defeated formation was the Syrian 68th Infantry Brigade, part of the 7th Infantry Division, a key element of the Syrian attack force of 6 to 7 October. The Syrian 7th had been embroiled in the 'Valley of Tears', and had been no less mauled than Israeli forces. The defeated Syrian brigade, however, was commanded by a Druze, Colonel Rafiq Hilawi. According to several sources, chiefly from which appears to be Israeli historian Chaim Herzog, Colonel Hilawi was paraded in a camp on the outskirts of Damascus where he was stripped of his badges of rank before facing a firing squad. It was this, if the report is true, and there are

A destroyed and now rusted Syrian tank in its fortified position overlooking Kibbutz Tel Katzir and the settlements on the Sea of Galilee. (Courtesy of GPO, Israel)

many who deny it, that assisted in stiffening the resolve of Syrian brigade and divisional commanders. They went on to fight the Israelis for every inch of territory yielded.

The offensive was characterised by small but ferocious battles fought on a village-by-village, and mile-by-mile basis, across dense minefields and against determined Syrian opposition. This was a far cry from the wide armoured sweeps and the set-piece formations that crushed the enemy and netted thousands of prisoners in 1967. These were short but bloody engagements that cost both sides significantly in armour and casualties. The Israelis gained territory in increments against camouflaged and emplaced Syrian armour and artillery, which were by no means in disarray, but fighting an organised rearguard action of interdiction and attrition.

Despite Israeli control of the air, occasional Syrian MiGs and Sukhoi fighter-bombers appeared overhead, offering Syrian ground units air support. It was a dispersed and fluid front that from the beginning, and for a considerable time afterwards, shifted steadily in the direction of the Israeli advance towards Damascus. On Friday, 12 October, Israeli forces broke into the village of Mazraat Beit Jinn, and after six hours of tank engagement, occupied the village and the surrounding hill country.

To the south, General Laner's division was moving parallel with Eitan's, and fighting the same battle of intense and dispersed engagements. The principal action was the taking of a fortified hill called Tel Shams, which was assaulted three times by armoured cavalry charge, and each time beaten back by infantry tank-killer squads armed with Saggers and RPGs. This action, in post-battle analysis, has tended to be regarded as a misuse of armour in an infantry role. This fact was borne out somewhat by the eventual capture of the position on 13 October by elements of the Israeli 31st Parachute Brigade led by Lieutenant Colonel Jonathan Netanyahu. Netanyahu would later gain immortality as the leader, and only fatality, of the iconic raid on Entebbe.

From there the Southern Division pressed on inland, encountering stiff opposition, but maintaining momentum along the Damascus road with slow but relentless progress. In the air, the Israeli air force was operating with its accustomed mastery of the skies, mounting deep penetration sorties to bomb Syrian airfields, fuel depots and power stations.

On 12 October, as the Northern Division was battling to take the Tel Shams, advance units of the Southern Division were probing eastwards towards the Village of Kanaker, no more than 15km from the western outskirts of Damascus. Laner's headquarters was established on a high position overlooking the approaches to Damascus, from where the movement of a large armoured force in the direction of the frontline caught his attention. After efforts to identify it, it was concluded that this was the long-expected Iraqi expeditionary force, now entering the field of battle from the southeast.

The division in question was the Iraqi 3rd Armoured Division, arriving piecemeal in Syria, and deploying towards the southern flank of Israeli forces. A brief, long-range encounter took place on the evening of the 12th, as the two divisions came within range of one another. As darkness fell, Laner predicted that the engagement would lead into a concentrated Iraqi assault mounted the following morning. Under the cover of darkness, he deployed his forces in an ambush-box position.The next morning, after some hesitation, the Iraqis deployed directly into it.

The Iraqis had been poorly briefed before entering the battle, and had only been superficially integrated into the overall Syrian defence. Their orders appear to have been no more detailed than to move forward to the front and fight.

An Israeli Air Force CH-53 Sikorsky helicopter with a command car slung underneath its belly. (Courtesy of GPO, Israel)

On 14 October, a detachment of Saudi Arabian troops was airlifted into Syria in six Iranian C-130 transport aircraft. The Saudi Arabian formation deployed in French Panhard armoured cars and was given the task of guarding the Damascus to Deraa road.

Thus, on 13 October, as the first light of dawn began to streak the sky, the leading Iraqi brigade was drawn into a topographical deadend, with the Israelis deployed along three sides and all guns directed inwards. The order to fire was given, and although accounts differ notably on the minutia of the battle, what is not arguable is the fact that the Iraqis were soon retreating under heavy fire, leaving behind at least eighty burning tanks in the killing field. The Israeli tanks then moved forward, leaving units of paratroopers behind to mop up in the surrounding hills.

This battle was without doubt an Israeli triumph. The Iraqis mounted no major operation after that, but the advent of Iraqi forces on the battlefield brought the general Israeli advance to a halt. On the western approaches to Damascus, Israeli howitzers established positions and began shelling a military airbase on the outskirts of the city.

A Jordanian division – a latecomer to the war – now reluctantly entered the battlefield on the side of the Syrians, but it mounted no notable attacks. The discovery of Western-supplied equipment by the Israelis during later inspections of the battlefield, suggested strongly that a Saudi Arabian force had also been present. Inter-Arab coordination was poor, however, and on the whole, Arab allied involvement had been too little too late.

The Israeli counter-offensive in the northern sector was a success, netting about three hundred square miles of Syrian territory. This effectively brought the war on the northern front to an end, a front upon which the Israelis admitted to the loss 772 men killed, 2,453 wounded and 65 taken prisoner. The Syrians subsequently acknowledged an unofficial casualty total of between 10,000 and 12,000, but gave no specific breakdown.

By then, international diplomatic manoeuvres were already underway to shape the future peace, and further Israeli advances into Syria were halted under pressure from the United States, and threats from the Soviet Union.

Syrian armed forces were on the verge of collapse, and the situation was desperate. Bold predictions of Syrian forces fighting to the death, even if Damascus fell, were aired in broadcasts that nonetheless began to appear increasingly shrill. Assad pleaded for assistance from every friendly power, but most

Yom Kippur War. An Israeli crewman with tank ammunition on the west bank of the Suez Canal. (Courtesy of GPO, Israel)

particularly, he began to apply pressure on the Egyptians to launch their long-mooted seizure of Israeli territory in the Sinai, and so take pressure off the Syrian army now battling for survival in the north.

Assad had in fact initially pressed Sadat to support a ceasefire quite early in the war, at a point when the Egyptians had successfully crossed the Suez Canal and occupied the east bank, and during Syria's brief occupation of the Golan Heights. Despite the war having satisfied his criteria for its launch, Sadat refused at that point to consider a ceasefire. His strategy then appeared to be to exhaust the Israelis in a campaign of attrition. Initially at least, this was proving successful.

Now, however, it was certainly too late for Assad to contemplate any such advantageous ceasefire, and he must bitterly have regretted not forcefully suing for a ceasefire a week earlier.

As early as 11 October, however, Sadat had begun receiving anguished diplomatic appeals from Assad to launch a major Egyptian assault in the Sinai. Sadat, while refusing a ceasefire, was also unwilling at that moment to commit to an extension of the war. The main point of consideration was the anti-aircraft shield, which enjoyed a limited reach, and beyond which Egyptian forces would be at the mercy of the IAF. The Arab effort in this war, however, although unbalanced and piecemeal, amounted to a coalition. If the Syrian and Egyptian cups did not runneth over with mutual cooperation, Arab financial and political support was no less important, and to abandon Syria would have undermined Egypt's national and Sadat's personal prestige.

Sadat then went on to make a fateful decision that would radically shift the balance of the war. On 12 October, he ordered a major push inland to seize the Gidi and Mitla passes, to begin the next day. This decision, however, caused major disagreements at Centre 10 in Cairo. Several times since the crossing, Shazly had advocated a lightning advance on the Sinai passes while the Israeli's were still shocked, and later as Russian resupply began to reach the Egyptian frontlines, before the Israelis could regain the initiative. On each occasion, however, General Ismail disagreed, partly due to the Israeli air threat, but also to ensure the consolidation of the bridgeheads before any ambitious forward movement. As early as 9 October, several senior Egyptian officers approached Ismail, also urging further movement inland as quickly as possible. A delay, they feared and advised, would simply transfer the initiative to the Israelis.

On 12 October, when procedural orders reached General Shazly, instructing him to commence the advance inland the following day, he resisted. The moment, he insisted, had passed. The Israelis had regained strength, confidence and control of the battlefield. The IAF was bristling for action, and as the Syrians were being rolled back across the Golan, the Israelis would now increasingly be able to focus their attention on the Sinai. After refusing three consecutive orders, Shazly responded only when ordered directly by Sadat. The date of the operation, however, was pushed forward a day, and set for 14 October.

In the Sinai, Israeli forces had now succeeded in stabilising the line, and in a series of low-level but intense engagements, the IDF began to get the measure of Egyptian tactics, developing means to deal with them. Some sort of a decisive movement was expected by the Israelis, who surmised that the Sinai passes would be the next Egyptian target. Discussion on

An Israeli Air Force Skyhawk comes in to land. (Courtesy of GPO, Israel)

the practicalities of an offensive crossing of the Canal went on, but it was decided that the risk presented to such an operation by two Egyptian reserve divisions deployed on the west side was too great. Until those divisions crossed to the east, where they could be lured into battle, the Israelis would continue to harass and probe the Egyptian bridgeheads.

A plan, nonetheless, began to form. Sharon's earlier reconnaissance probe had revealed the seam between the Second and Third Egyptian armies, corresponding on the opposite bank with the Egyptian city of Deversoir. An additional advantage of contemplating a crossing at this point was the cover offered on the left flank by the Great Bitter Lake. Prefabricated bridging equipment was assembled and placed on standby. Pressure to move immediately – there was a great deal of this – originated from Sharon, who continued to be a thorn in the side of the sectoral command.

The decision to go ahead, however, lay not with the sectoral command, but with the chiefs of staff. In Tel Aviv on the evening of the 12th, a meeting was held to discuss the matter. During this meeting, there was some disagreement between Elazar and Dayan. Dayan expressed reservations in regards to the operation as a whole, but, accepting a consensus against him, he presented the matter for the consideration of the prime minister and her cabinet. Here too, there was considerable scepticism over the feasibility of the operation, and the likelihood of it forcing the Egyptians to accept a ceasefire.

There can be no doubt that an operation such as this was maverick and risky, but it conformed very much to the IDF self-image. It was this that no doubt inspired Sharon to advocate for it as forcefully as he did.

In the end, Elazar agreed that no decision would be made until a complete Egyptian deployment to the east bank had taken place. Then, as the meeting was ending, an intelligence brief was handed to Elazar indicating that the movement of the Egyptian reserve divisions across the Suez had in fact begun. This stirred an immediate reaction. Clearly, the long-expected Egyptian assault was imminent. The question of an Israeli crossing of the Suez now became de facto. It would take place, but not until the IDF had broken the back of Egyptian armour.

Yom Kippur War. Damaged Egyptian tanks abandoned in the desert in the Sinai. (Courtesy of GPO, Israel)

10. SNATCHING DEFEAT FROM THE JAWS OF VICTORY

I have been fighting for twenty-five years, and all the rest were just battles. This was a real war.

(Ariel Sharon)

With the news of the movement of Egyptian reserve armour across the canal, all attention shifted to the Sinai.

The settlement of the war was always likely to be in this theatre, and the Israelis were ready for it. Conversely, a deep sense of apprehension lay at the heart of the Egyptian command. Sadat had been coerced into ordering the advance, and General Shazly, the Egyptian GOC, only very reluctantly accepted the order. Then, having been overruled by executive order, Shazly succeeded only in postponing the offensive from 13 to 14 October. The movement of heavy armour across the canal alerted the Israelis to what was afoot, as did probing Egyptian attacks all along the line during the 13th. The Egyptian plan, as it was hastily formalised, was for an armoured advance in a wide pincer movement with the objective of capturing the Israeli southern command nerve centre at Refidim. An armoured division and an armoured brigade would advance from the area of the Gidi Pass crossroads, along the Lateral Road midway between the southern shore of the Great Bitter Lake and the northern apex of the Gulf of Suez, while a second arm of the pincer would comprise an armoured division launching from the area of Ismailia–Deversoir.

The IDF Southern Command deployed in expectation of a wide frontal attack, with large blocking forces at either end of the Suez. It was anticipated that the IAF would lead the battle once Egyptian forces had emerged from their anti-aircraft shield. Should the main Egyptian effort be concentrated in the centre, however, Sharon's and Mandler's divisions would hold it. If the assault struck in the direction of Refidim, Adan's division, alongside elements of Sharon's division, would be held in reserve to attack the Egyptians on their flank.

Both operational plans were simple and to the point, reflecting the raw elements of tank warfare on a battlefield where mobile desert warfare utilising armour and armoured infantry had been incubated. This set the stage for one of the greatest series of tank battles of history.

On the morning of 13 October General Mandler was killed when his voice, in a radio conversation with Elazar, was identified by Egyptian electronic warfare units using tactical COMINT equipment. His position was immediately transmitted to the nearest Second Army artillery battery that opened fire on his position.

Above: Yom Kippur War. Destroyed armour abandoned on the west bank of the Suez Canal. (Courtesy of GPO, Israel)

Right: Yom Kippur War. Wounded Israeli soldiers being treated in the Sinai. (Courtesy of GPO, Israel)

It is hard to imagine a more ill-conceived battlefield strategy than the Egyptian attack of 14 October 1973. Its motivations were political, and were from the onset; it was a suicidal departure from the cautious but innovative tactics that had brought the Egyptians to such a commanding initial position. There can be no doubt that, had the thrust inland been undertaken two or three days earlier, the result would have been very different. Bearing in mind the knife-edge balance upon which the northern front hung at that time, a comprehensive Israeli defeat in the Sinai would certainly have changed the course of the war.

In the event, however, the Egyptian armoured brigades emerged from under the cover of their anti-aircraft shield, and rushed headlong into carefully prepared IDF positions. Covered by withering IAF ground support, the next few decisive but heavily contested hours saw the virtual destruction of the Egyptian armoured capability. The Egyptians opened the attack with a heavy artillery barrage, after which, between 6.00am and 8.00am, ground forces moved into action.

In the north, the Egyptian 18th Infantry Division, stiffened by a tank brigade equipped with Soviet T-62 tanks, moved out from the area of El Quantara towards Rumani along the main Mediterranean road. Egyptian commando units were deployed by helicopter into an extensive area of salt marsh in advance of Rumani. Here Israeli lines were somewhat over-extended. It was also the last hold-out among the Bar Lev fortifications – the Budapest position. Adan was ordered to direct his division north to take on the Egyptians, and within a few hours, the Egyptian advance had been halted and thrown back with the loss of some fifty tanks. In the meanwhile, hurtling into the arms of Sharon's division came the unfortunate Egyptian 21st Armoured Division (crossed from the west bank that morning), supported by a tank brigade from the 23rd Mechanised Division. The Israelis allowed the Egyptians to come into close range, engaging at ranges at times as close as 75m, and in a confused and murderous melee, the Egyptians were annihilated, and thrown back with the loss of a reported ninety-three tanks. The Egyptian 1st Mechanised Brigade was almost destroyed, at the cost to the Israelis of just three tanks hit by missile fire.

To the south, two Egyptian tank brigades attempted to break through to the Gidi and Mitla passes, but were stopped by Mandler's division, now commanded by Brigadier General Kalman Magen, in a manner somewhat less decisive, but ultimately successful, claiming from the Egyptians upwards of sixty tanks.

Parallel to this effort, a special Egyptian task force, comprising an infantry and tank brigade, assumed a southerly push along the Gulf of Suez in an attempt to effect a deep flanking

At the onset of the Battle of the Sinai, Israeli aircraft entered Egyptian airspace to launch pre-emptive strikes against Egyptian installations. The principal Israeli target was the Egyptian airbase at El Mansoura in the Nile delta. Something of this sort was expected, and several Egyptian MiG-21s were on standby at the end of the airfield with pilots ready for immediate take-off. Twenty Israeli Phantoms were intercepted, later joined by more, as well as several Skyhawk fighters, and a major air battle ensued. Following the war, the IAF admitted that seventeen Israeli aircraft had been shot down for the loss of six MiG-21s.

Yom Kippur War. Prime Minister Golda Meir and cabinet members visiting the Southern Command in the Sinai. (Courtesy of GPO, Israel)

movement from the south against the Mitla Pass. This force was engaged, and largely wiped out by Israeli paratroop forces and tanks holding the pass. The survivors attempted to retreat southwards, but were engaged by the IAF, and, upon retreating eventually back under cover of the anti-aircraft shield, could count the loss of some ninety tanks.

By the evening of 14 October, Egyptian forces were ordered back to the cover of their bridgeheads, deeply shocked by what had all along been predicted would be a total disaster. A brief hiatus followed as the Israelis waited for the expected follow-up, but the Egyptians were beaten.

The Israelis counter-attacked in the north, liberating the bitterly contested Budapest fortification. Thereafter, they pondered a battlefield upon which 264 destroyed Egyptian tanks were counted, with an estimated loss of 1,000 personnel, all at the cost of just ten Israeli tanks. These were the sorts of results to which the Israelis had become accustomed. With the balance of the battlefield now very much in their favour, thought began to be given to the long-advocated counter-crossing, and the final, decisive punch of the war.

The battle of 14 October proved in the end to be the decisive moment. At its immediate conclusion, Shazly advised that the Egyptian armoured reserved be returned across the canal, effectively ruling out any further offensive action. This was overruled by Ismail, again for political reasons, for this would have been construed as a retreat, and therefore a defeat. This, again, would prove itself disastrous, and Shazly was apt in later interviews and writings to acknowledge this. A concentrated assault in divisional strength against the key points of the Sinai passes would have almost certainly succeeded better than a wide frontal assault along 100km of front, into pre-prepared Israeli positions.

Yom Kippur War. *Aluf* Arik Sharon at a bridge built by the Israeli army engineers over the Suez Canal. (Courtesy of GPO, Israel)

The Israeli high command was quick to grasp the truth that the tide of war had shifted. In her memoir, *My Life*, Golda Meir, remembering a meeting with David Elazar soon after the results of the battle were known, recorded Elazar's relieved comments: 'Golda, he said, 'it will be alright. We are back to ourselves and they [the Egyptians] are back to themselves.'

And indeed, this was true.

Elazar then judged the moment right to release Israeli casualty figures to date on the Sinai front – 656 known dead, including General Avraham Mandler, commander of the 252nd Armoured Division. Despite significantly greater Egyptian losses, the smaller Israeli population experienced a far greater per-capita loss, and the fact was sobering indeed.

Later that evening, Elazar approached cabinet for approval of the plan to cross to the west bank, an operation codenamed *Abirey-Halev* (Stout-hearted Men). Approval was granted soon after midnight on 15 October, the day after the Egyptian defeat. The plan, again, was essentially simple. An Israeli armoured division would cross the Suez at the junction between the Egyptian Second (north) and Third (south) armies with a view to encircling the western

The Israelis were by then armed with sophisticated anti-tank missiles, including TOW (Tube Launched, Optically Tracked, Wire-guided) missiles supplied by the United States.

flank of the Third Army by the capture of the Egyptian city of Suez. This would effectively cut off the Third Army from retreat into Egypt proper, and isolate it from resupply. This would grant Israel a very strong hand in any future peace process, and would most certainly bring about an end to the war. At that point, the Israelis were fielding a force of just over 700 tanks, distributed among four divisions, commanded individually by generals Sharon, Adan, Magen and Sasson.

The first phase of the operation was to clear and secure road access to the proposed crossing point, and then secure the Israeli right flank, which would be the southern flank of the Second Army bridgehead. Over preceding years, the IDF had prepared a platform for a potential crossing of the Suez Canal within the framework of normal military planning. This position happened to coincide with the seam between the Egyptian Second Army and Third Army bridgeheads, with the additional advantage of having on the Israeli left flank, the cover of the Great Bitter Lake.

The task of securing both sides of the canal fell to Sharon's division. This entailed expanding the secure area, encompassing the points known as the Chinese Farm and Missouri, and the two roads that approached the crossing point on the east bank – Akavish and Tirtur. General Adan would then cross the Canal with his 162nd Armoured Division to take out the surrounding Egyptian air-defence system, opening airspace for the IAF to begin interdiction. Sharon would then be relieved by the 252nd Armoured Division, commanded by Magen, allowing him to cross, and then disperse to provide flank coverage for Adan's southward push to take the city of Suez. To support the operation, Elazar added the additional component of a paratroop force inserted by helicopter.

The operation opened on 15 October at 5.00pm, and almost immediately one of the most costly and brutal battles of the war was triggered. The forces threatening the Israeli advance to the canal formed the southern flank of the Second Army. Units here comprised an Egyptian armoured division (the 21st) and an infantry division (the 16th). The terrain was open desert with two roads converging at a point on the east bank opposite Deversoir. It was these, as well as a 5km-deep buffer, that Sharon was ordered to secure. His plan called for a diversionary attack from the east, mounted by a brigade commanded by Colonel Tuvia Raviv, while a second brigade, commanded by Colonel Haim Erez, would bring in the prefabricated bridge.

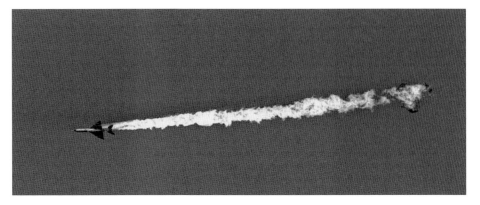

Yom Kippur War. An Egyptian MiG-21 in flames after taking an Israeli hit over the west bank of the Suez Canal. The pilot can be seen to have bailed out. (Courtesy of GPO, Israel)

Yom Kippur War. The struck Egyptian MiG crashes into the ground. (Courtesy of GPO, Israel)

Yom Kippur War. An Israeli tank crew laying the injured Egyptian pilot of the shot-down MiG on a stretcher. (Courtesy of GPO, Israel)

Colonel Amon Reshef's 14th Armoured Brigade would then take on the critical task of driving up against the Egyptian Second Army's southern flank in order to secure the crossing point. No one anticipated that this would be easy, and accordingly Reshef's brigade was reinforced by four armoured and three mechanised infantry battalions, joined by a reconnaissance battalion – the 87th Armoured Reconnaissance Battalion, commanded by Lieutenant Colonel Yoav Brom.

The Battle for Chinese Farm, as the encounter has since come to known, began at 7.00pm as Reshef set off on his mission. With the 87th in the lead, the brigade moved into the gap, after which it swung north, moving parallel with the Canal. At a point about 3km north of Deversoir, it ran into Egyptian defensive positions, rousing the Egyptian 16th Infantry Division, and mobilising immediate resistance. Thereafter, and for several days to follow, a close-range and confused tank and infantry battle raged in the open desert. At the end of the next day's fighting, Reshef's tank force had been whittled down from ninety-six to forty-one tanks.

Ariel Sharon would later recall, writing in his memoirs, *Warrior*:

> The morning of October 6 dawned on the most terrible sight I have ever seen. All that night Ammon's brigade, along with several paratrooper elements, the remnants of Yoav Brom's reconnaissance unit, one of Tuvia's battalions and one of Haim Erez's, had been engaged with the better part of two Egyptian divisions.

The scene was nightmarish. The battle had taken place in a relatively limited geographic area, and within that area lay the smoking ruins of at least fifty Israeli tanks and three times that number of Egyptian ones. Debris littered the desert, while black smoke hung in a heavy pall over the scene, thick with the stench of blood and explosives. The Israelis lost 300 dead and many more wounded, while Egyptian losses, undisclosed, were much heavier. Fighting would continue with the Israelis, incurring ongoing losses in men and equipment as they fought for every inch of territory yielded by the Egyptians.

As this battle was ongoing, the first Israeli troops began crossing the Canal. Infantry and tanks crossed in inflatables and rafts, moving immediately to establish a 5km-wide bridgehead on the west bank. This was a bold opening move, because access to the staging area had yet to be secured. Added to this, an uncertain battle still raged to the north, the roads remaining closed to the necessary bridging equipment for the full-scale movement of an expeditionary force. The risk was that the initial force might find itself trapped and cut off, which would, under the circumstances, have been a military and political disaster.

The priority then became to clear the roads and establish a secure position to complete the crossing. The Egyptian Second Army was reinforced along its southern flank, and, notwithstanding the new tide of the war and the Israeli threat to the Egyptian rear, the Egyptians fought with resolve and great determination. Additional Israeli armour and infantry were also committed to the operation, but it quickly became obvious that neither side would yield the position without a fight. Upon control of Chinese Farm pivoted the survival of each side. For reasons both soldierly and political, the Israelis could not abandon their isolated bridgehead in Egypt. At the same time, a successful Israeli crossing would trap huge numbers of Egyptians on the west bank, which would mark an effective Egyptian defeat.

Yom Kippur War. Egyptian prisoners of war, some barefoot, being taken to an Israeli base on the west bank of the Suez Canal. (Courtesy of GPO, Israel)

Yom Kippur War. Israeli soldiers at their observation post on the west bank of the Suez Canal. On the parapet, loaded and ready to use, the Belgium-made FN MAG (Mitrailleuse d'Appui Général) 7.62 mm-calibre, general-purpose machine gun. (Courtesy of GPO, Israel)

Thus, the battle raged. Nevertheless, five days of intense and bloody fighting, brutally destructive to both sides, in the end proved more destructive to the Egyptians. With tanks depleted and troops exhausted, the Egyptian 16th Infantry Brigade finally abandoned its positions, relinquishing the Chinese Farm to the Israelis, and in doing so, finally opening the road to an organised crossing.

On the night of 17–18 October, a bridge was established, and the Israeli divisions began to cross. The operation was now poised to proceed along its original plan, although now Adan would advance southwards towards the Egyptian city of Suez, encircling the rear of the Egyptian Third Army, and threatening to cut it off. Sharon would at the same time move northwards in the direction of the city of Ismaili, which would, if not entirely isolate, then certainly compromise the Egyptian Second Army.

Again, however, the Israelis encountered firmer than expected resistance from the Egyptians. Whilst the realisation was quickly dawning on the Egyptians that they faced a massive reversal, they would suffer a wholesale defeat if some diplomatic wrench was not thrown in the wheel of Israeli forward momentum.

Efforts to this end were, very much underway, but for the time being, standing now as they did upon the cusp of victory, the Israelis too were beginning to count the cost. General Adan was forging a slow advance south, which meant he could now predict an encirclement of Suez, but not its occupation. Egyptian resistance remained formidable, and in the face of it, the Israelis continued to sustain losses in men and materiel. There were many in Israel now asking why, when the war was effectively won, was the IDF still sacrificing men in a non-essential extension of operations.

Yom Kippur War. Israeli troops dug in on the west bank of the Suez Canal. (Courtesy of GPO, Israel)

The situation, however, had by then reached its tipping point. The Egyptian command was beginning to crumble, and resistance increasingly began to take on the character of isolated and dilatory actions that hindered rather than threatened to halt the Israeli advance.

In Cairo, as the battle for Chinese Farm raged on, and as the Israelis established a bridgehead on the west bank, an antipathy, that had been simmering since the first days of the war between General Shazly and his cabinet superior General Ismail, erupted into open conflict. Shazly advised the withdrawal of four armoured brigades from the east to the west bank to confront the Israeli advance against Suez, to which Ismail refused, repeating Sadat's insistence that no territory on the west bank be relinquished. This, he said, might spark a panic, but more importantly, events had convinced Sadat that he now needed a ceasefire more than the Israelis did. When Shazly appealed directly to Sadat, the latter stepped into the argument on the side of his minister of war. No forces, he confirmed, would be withdrawn from the east to the west bank.

11. WAR, THE INSTRUMENT OF POLITICS

Peace will come when the Arabs love their children more than they hate us.

(Golda Meir)

As Egypt began to stagger under the weight of the Israeli resurgence, other Arab countries reacted in support.

On 17 October, a day after Sadat appealed to the Soviet Union to convene the United Nation Security Council to secure a ceasefire, the Arab oil-producing states raised the price of oil by seventy per cent. They also threatened five per cent cut in production for every month that Israel remained in the territories occupied during the Six-Day War.

The next day, on 18 October, the Saudi government went further. It announced a ten per cent cut in oil output, and when, a day later, US President Richard Nixon formally requested Congress to authorise a $2.2 billion emergency aid package for Israel, Saudi Arabia responded by placing an oil embargo on the United States. Other Arab countries soon followed. The market ramifications were unthinkable, and Nixon was obliged, in the midst of the Watergate scandal, to divert his full attention to the Middle East crisis. What this meant in practical terms was that Secretary of State Henry Kissinger would cease to block UN ceasefire efforts, and now take the lead in securing a viable ceasefire on behalf of the Israelis.

Yom Kippur War. A long column of Israeli paratroopers, troops and vehicles winds its way along the Suez–Cairo road on the west bank of the Suez Canal. (Courtesy of GPO, Israel)

Yom Kippur War. A motorised Israeli patrol passes through damaged and abandoned Egyptian tanks and trucks along the Ismailia–Cairo Road. (Courtesy of GPO, Israel)

On 19 October, Kissinger accepted an invitation from the Soviet leadership, delivered in the most convoluted diplomatic language imaginable, to visit Moscow in order to discuss means of ending hostilities. By the next day, 20 October, Sadat had been briefed that both superpowers were throwing their weight behind a ceasefire, and it was in this context, primarily, that he refused to countenance an Egyptian withdrawal from the east bank.

Kissinger wasted no time, and by 22 October the terms of a ceasefire had broadly been agreed to by the two superpowers. Kissinger then travelled to Israel to present the plan to the Israeli cabinet while Soviet premier, Alexei Kosygin, made his way to Cairo to deliver Sadat more or less the same message. These visits were, superficially at least, described as consultative, but neither side in the war could, nor perhaps would have, contested a ceasefire. While threats and counter-threats continued to reverberate over the battlefield, for the most part both sides froze their positions in place and waited.

On 22 October 1973, the Israeli cabinet formally accepted the ceasefire, but no less formally committed the IDF to punishing the Egyptians for any violations. In fact, infuriated at being held back within striking distance of Suez, it was the Israeli advance column that felt the greater pressure to continue hostilities.

On 22 October, Israeli Prime Minister Golda Meir, anxious to complete the encirclement of the Egyptian Third Army before operations ceased, tacitly granted permission for the advance to continue. This gained the desired isolation of the Egyptian Third Army, but stirred such shrill appeals from Cairo that, after a brief exchange of accusation and counter-accusation, a second ceasefire came into effect on 25 October. This was followed very quickly by the

Yom Kippur War. Israeli troops in half-tracks patrol the countryside on the west bank of the Suez Canal. (Courtesy of GPO, Israel)

deployment of a United Nations monitoring force, and in due course, under international pressure, the Israelis partially lifted the siege of Suez City, allowing UN relief supplies to reach the civilian population. The Egyptian Third Army, however, was still cut off and isolated, and local and international tension remained high as the plight of trapped Egyptians troops grew acute. The Soviets uttered threats, and placed airborne units on alert. Brezhnev assured his US counterpart that the Soviet Union would not shy from despatching troops to the Middle East, unilaterally if necessary, to ensure Israeli compliance with the ceasefire. The United States responded with a Condition III alert of its own armed forces, the highest since the Cuban Missile Crisis, which the Soviet Union took note of. A de-escalation followed, but the point was made.

On the frontline, however, tensions remained high. The Egyptian Third Army was encircled, but the Second Army was still intact. In general, Egyptian ground forces remained both in position and under orders. The question now remained: what could be achieved by the Arab belligerents under the terms of this ceasefire? On the Golan, there was little to be salvaged. The Syrians had lost the territory, and there was slight hope now of negotiating its return.

Sharon also attempted to press on to capture Ismailia, but was thwarted by Egyptian military and international diplomatic resistance.

Yom Kippur War. Smoke billows over an Egyptian town across the Suez Canal following an Israeli bombardment. (Courtesy of GPO, Israel)

Syria, therefore, remained staunchly opposed to a peace process, which marked the formal end of the Egyptian-Syrian alliance.

In the end, disengagement of forces agreements between Egypt, Syria and Israel were only signed with Egypt on 18 January and Syria on 31 May 1974, three months after the effective end of hostilities. Only then did the IDF stand down, and demobilise its reserves.

To understand the peace that followed, it is necessary to spend a moment evaluating the impact of the war on Israel in particular. The world at large, and western military establishments in general, awarded Israel an outright victory in the war of 1973. In those quarters, at least, the Israeli military myth was untarnished. The Israelis had been taken by surprise, that much was true, and beaten almost to the canvas, but they had rallied, and returned to the fight to shame both Arab belligerents with a sound thrashing. However, at home the Israelis themselves tended to be more circumspect. Over 2,800 Israelis lost their lives, with three times that number wounded, and around 500 taken as prisoners of war. On a small population, this loss was keenly felt, and the Israeli post-mortem of the period involved a great deal of self-searching.

How had it happened that the intelligence establishment had been taken so unawares? This preamble to the war came to be known as *machdal*, or the blunder, and when the Agranat Commission released its findings, the finger of blame was pointed unequivocally at senior members of the Israeli intelligence community, in particular at the Director General for military intelligence, General Eli Zei'ra, whose career was thereafter terminated. The commission also found fault with General David Elazar, which surprised many analysts. This so shocked Elazar himself, that he retired from the military soon afterwards in embittered mood. He died three years later as he was composing his memoirs. While Elazar was reprimanded for over-confidence and arrogance, General Gonen, a hero of past campaigns, suffered harsh criticism for his lack of dynamism and ineffective command. While Gonen was certainly the most severely censured IDF officer, others were singled out too, including Sharon. While the military deflected some criticism by claiming that military men had been scapegoated to protect the political leadership – most notably Dayan – this did not stop the commanders themselves pointing the finger at one another in what later became known as the 'War of the Generals'.

Perhaps the most import impact of the war on the Israeli psyche, however, was to explode the myth of the IDF's own invincibility, to shock the nation out of some of its complacency and, as Sadat anticipated, to prompt the Israeli political and general establishment to view negotiations with the Arabs in a more favourable light.

The flag of the United Nations flies over the landing stage for amphibious tanks ferrying relief supplies to the Egyptian Third Army. (Courtesy of GPO, Israel)

On 6 November 1973, US Secretary of State Henry Kissinger made his first visit to Cairo, establishing a degree of entente that amply rewarded Sadat's initial interest in entering the US sphere of influence. Sadat accepted the notion of a separate peace unallied to wider Arab positions on Israel. He was subsequently party to long negotiations through many phases that resulted ultimately in the Camp David accords of September 1978. This important Middle East diplomatic milestone followed twelve days of secret negotiations at the presidential retreat of Camp David, arbitrated by US president Jimmy Carter. The outcome was a peace treaty signed by Anwar Sadat and Israeli prime minister of the moment, Menachem Begin.

Syria admitted to 3,500 fatalities. Egyptian losses are unknown, although the Israeli Knesset website claims 15,000.

Egyptian President Anwar Sadat listens to former Israeli prime minister Golda Meir, with Shimon Peres on the right, at a meeting of the Alignment Faction in the Israeli Knesset (parliament) on 21 November 1977, during Sadat's historic visit to Jerusalem. (Courtesy of GPO, Israel)

The key points of the Camp David accords called for:

- a formal peace treaty to be signed between Israel and Egypt, within three months
- establishment of diplomatic relations between the two countries
- Israeli withdrawal from the Sinai Peninsula in stages, to be completed within three years
- further meetings to resolve the Palestinian question. The meeting would include Jordan and a representative of the Palestinian people
- a five-year transitional period of Israeli withdrawal from the West Bank and Gaza (this transitional period would include the introduction of Palestinian self-government)
- an end to Israeli settlements in the West Bank

The accords, however, did not settle the question of East Jerusalem.

For this, Anwar Sadat suffered the approbation of Arab leaders, but, in spite of the Egyptian military shaming, Sadat at least proved, in an act of Clausewitzian brilliance, that war is an instrument of politics.

The Israelis withdrew from the Sinai, and although the Golan, Gaza and the West Bank remain occupied, Sadat could at least claim that his war objectives had been realised. The normalisation of relations between Israel and Egypt went into effect in January 1980, ambassadors were exchanged and scheduled airline flights began. The Sinai was demilitarised, and on 25 April 1982, Israel withdrew the last of her troops.

By this time, Ariel Sharon was Israeli defence minister, and displaying his clear contempt for the move, he let it to be known that this would be the last territorial concession Israel

Israeli armour causing a traffic jam while waiting to cross the causeway from the west bank to the eastern side of the Suez Canal at the third stage of disengagement. (Courtesy of GPO, Israel)

Israeli soldiers loading up landmines before the evacuation of the west bank of the Suez Canal. (Courtesy of GPO, Israel)

First Anniversary
memorial service of the
end of the Yom Kippur
War at the Kiryat Shaoul
military cemetery, Tel Aviv.

would make for peace. He promised a new Israeli settlement drive in the occupied West
Bank and the Gaza Strip.

As remarked by the *New York Times*, 'The turnover of the 7,500 square miles of territory,
representing the last third of the peninsula, was accomplished without fanfare, as a
reflection of Israeli sadness and disquiet.'

By then, Egyptian President Anwar Sadat had been dead for six months, assassinated in
1981 during a victory parade held in Cairo to commemorate the opening phase of Operation
Badr. His death came about consequent to a *fatwā* (an Islamic legal pronouncement, issued
by an expert in religious law) approving his assassination, which was carried by members of
the Egyptian Islamic Jihad. He was accused of betraying the Arab cause by recognising and
making peace with Israel.

Segen (lieutenant) Eli Cohen lowers the flag of Israel as troops complete the withdrawal from the west bank of the Suez Canal. (Courtesy of GPO, Israel)

SELECTED BIBLIOGRAPHY

Blum, Howard, *The Eve of Destruction*, Harper Collins, 2009.

Dan, Uri, *Ariel Sharon: An Intimate Portrait*, reprint edition, Griffin, 2007.

Dayan, Moshe, *The Story of my Life*, William Morrow and Company, 1976.

Gawrych, Dr, George W. *The 1973 Arab Israeli War*, Pickle Partners Publishing, 2015.

Herzog, Chaim, *Arab-Israeli Wars*, Vintage, 2004.

Herzog, Chaim, *The War of Atonement*, Weidenfeld and Nicolson, 1975.

Meir, Golda, *My Life*, Cox and Wyman Ltd, 1975.

Meir, Golda, *My Life*, Weidenfeld and Nicolson, 1975.

O'Ballance, Edgar, *No Victor, No Vanquished*, Presidio Press, 1996.

Rabinovich, Abraham, *The Yom Kippur War*, Schocken Books, 2004.

Shalev, Aryeh, *Israel's Intelligence Assessment before the Yom Kippur War*, Sussex Academic Press, 2010.

Sharon, Ariel, *Warrior: An Autobiography*, Simon & Shuster, 2005.

ABOUT THE AUTHOR

Peter Baxter is an author, amateur historian, and African field, mountain and heritage travel guide. Born in Kenya and educated in Zimbabwe, he has lived and travelled over much of southern and central Africa. He has guided in all the major mountain ranges south of the equator, helping develop the concept of sustainable travel, and the touring of battlefield and heritage sites in East Africa. Peter lives in Oregon, USA, working on the marketing of African heritage travel as well as a variety of book projects. His interests include British imperial history in Africa and the East Africa campaign of the First World War in particular.